BIRD

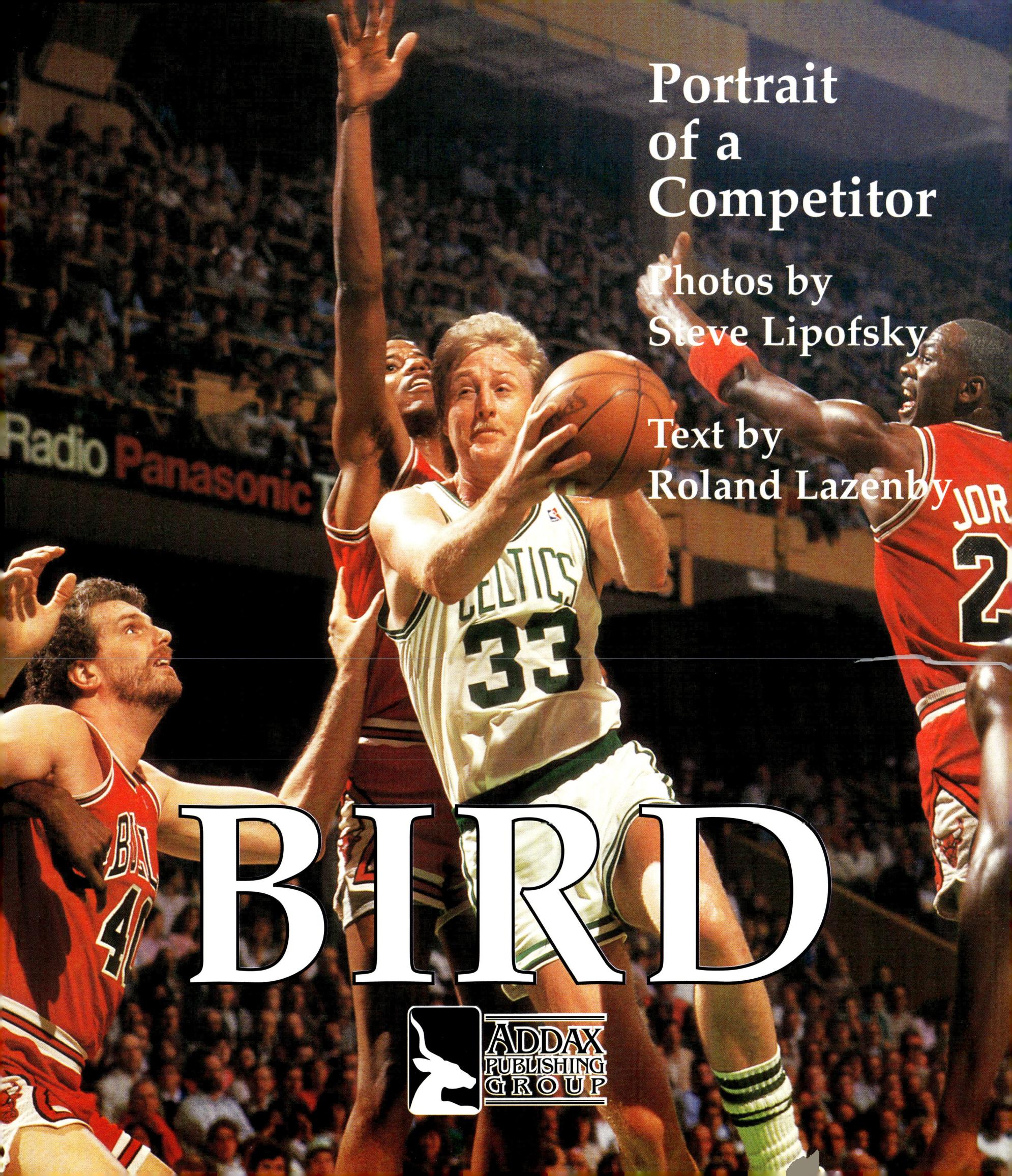

Portrait of a Competitor

Photos by Steve Lipofsky

Text by Roland Lazenby

ADDAX PUBLISHING GROUP

Published by Addax Publishing Group
Copyright © 1998 by Steve Lipofsky
and Roland Lazenby
Designed by Randy Breeden
Cover Design by Jerry Hirt
Edited by Susan Storey

"All photos herein shot on KODAK Professional Film"

All rights reserved. No part of this book may be reproduced or transmitted in any form or by any means, electronic or mechanical, including photocopying, recording, or by any information storage and retrieval system, without the written permission of the Publisher.
For Information address:
Addax Publishing Group
8643 Hauser Drive, Suite 235, Lenexa, KS 66215

ISBN: 1-886110-30-1

Distributed to the trade by
Andrews McMeel Publishing
4520 Main Street
Kansas City, MO 64111

1 3 5 7 9 10 8 6 4 2
Printed in Canada

Library of Congress Cataloging-in-Publication Data

Lipofsky, Steve
    Bird : portrait of a competitor / photos by Steve Lipofsky ; text by Roland Lazenby.
    p. cm.
    ISBN 1-886110-39-5
    1. Bird, Larry, 1956- —Pictorial works. 2. Basketball players--United States—Biography. 3. Basketball players—United States--Biography—Pictorial works. 4. Boston Celtics (Basketball team)
    I. Lazenby, Roland. II. Title.
GV884.B57L56 1998
796.323'092—dc21
[B]
                            98-12221
                              CIP

VISITOR
BOSTON
83 4 86
PLAYER PENALTY
9 26
BOSTON CELTICS
PISTONS

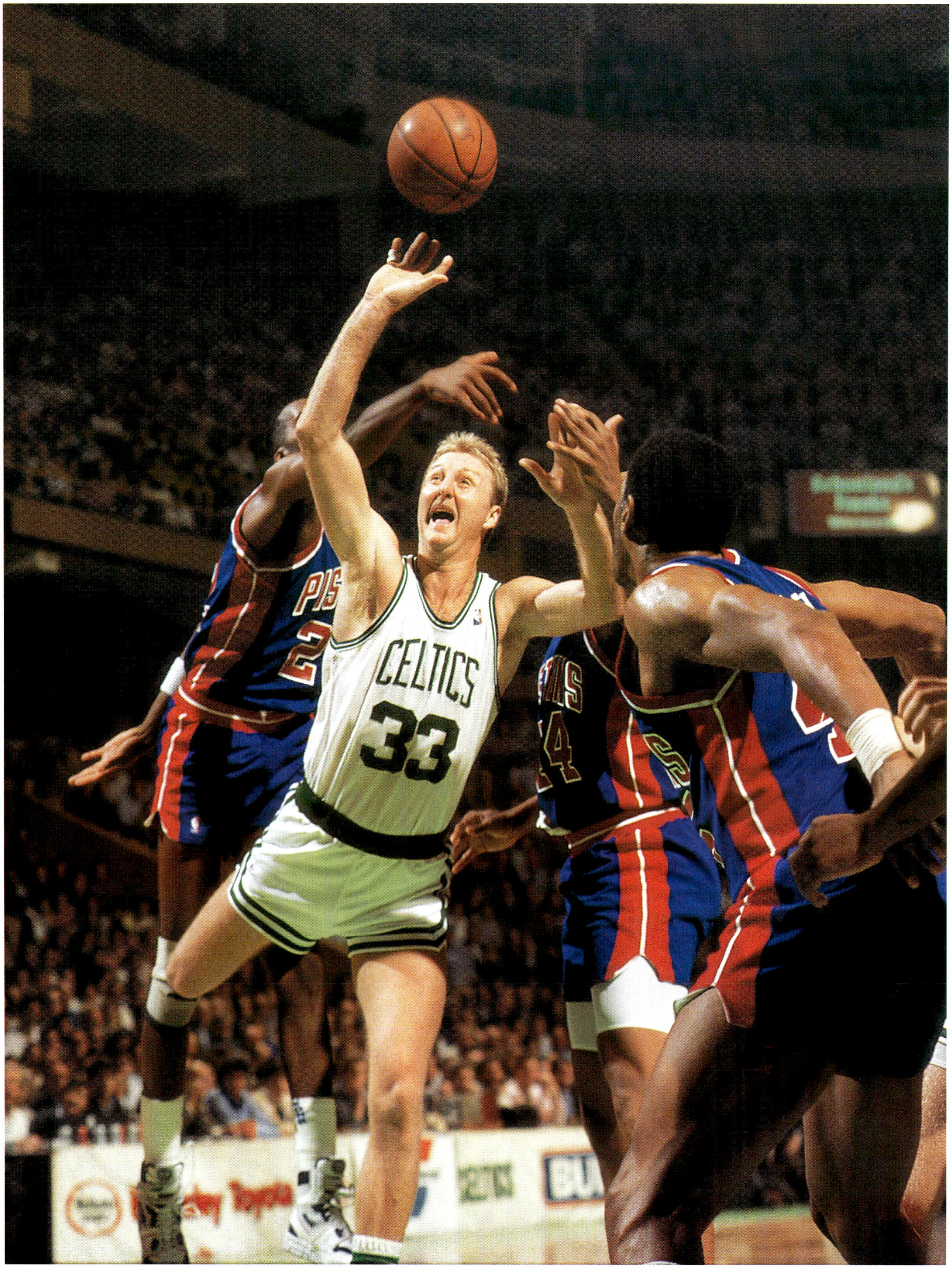
CELTICS
33

Contents

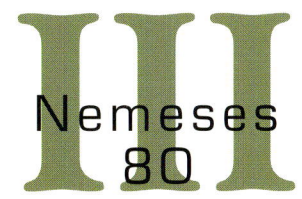

I
Indiana Gothic
11

II
Garden Glory
30

III
Nemeses
80

IV
Playing With Pain
90

V
Letting Go
98

VI
Indiana
108

VII
Stats
118

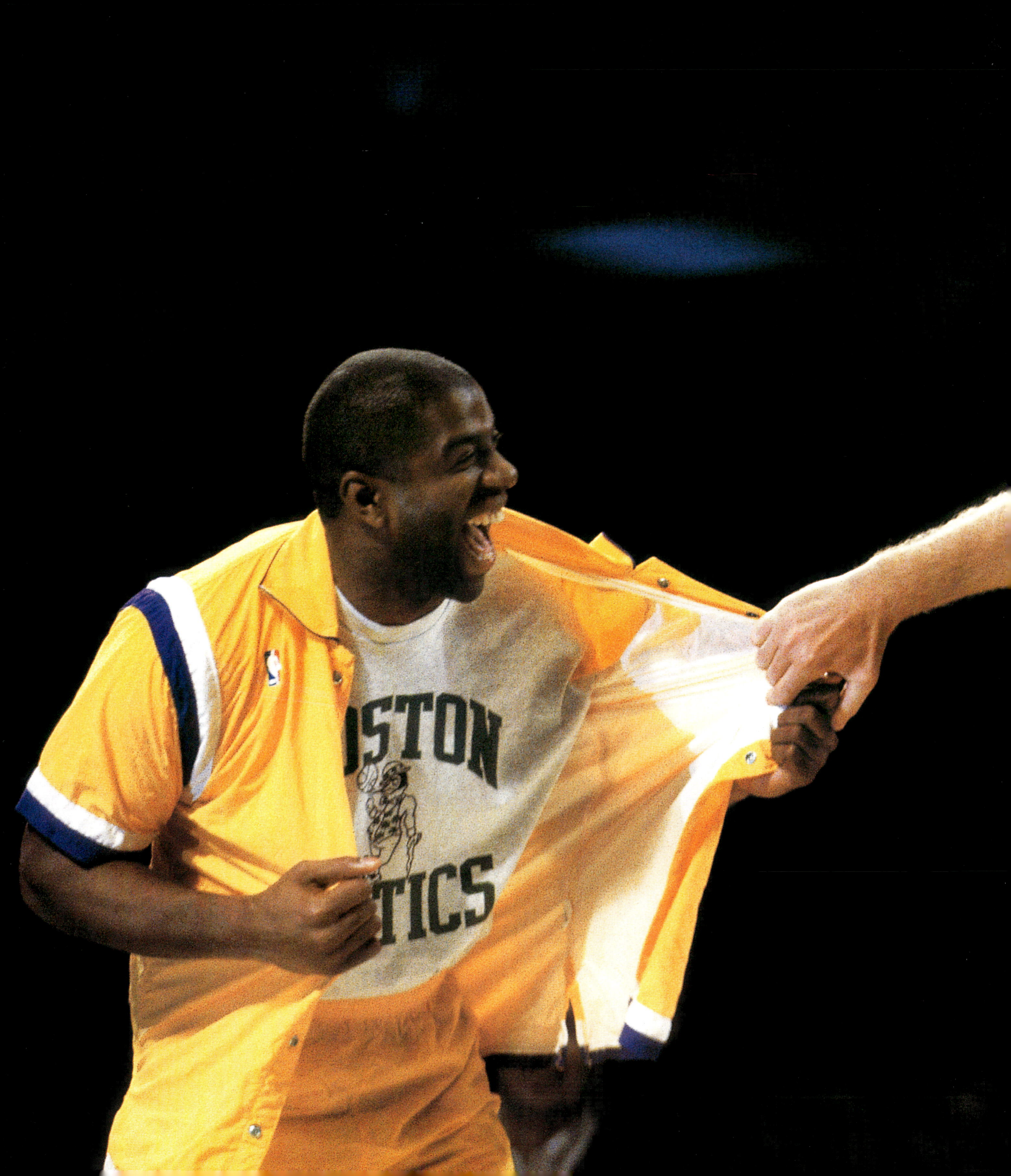
OSTON
TICS

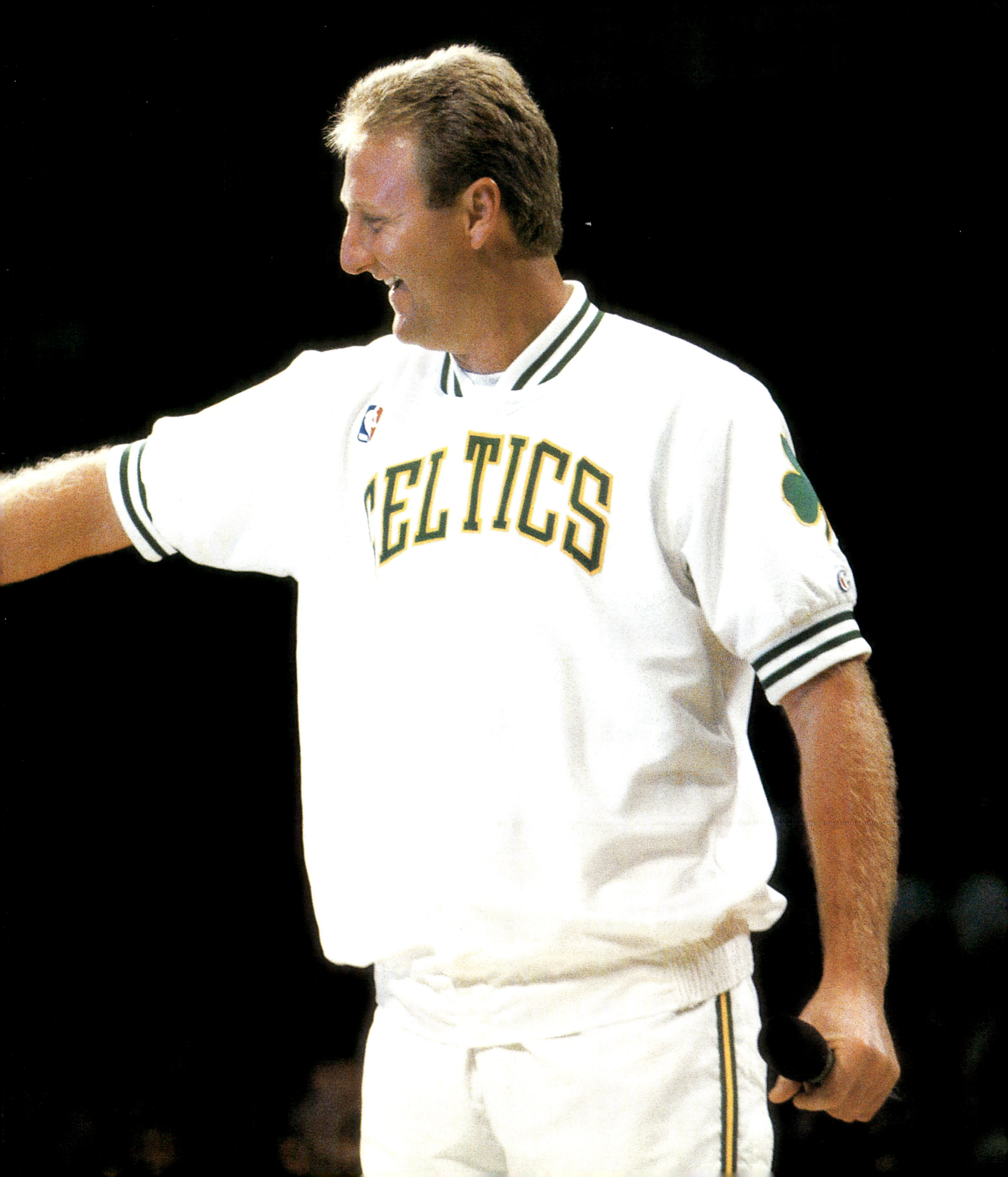

ELTICS

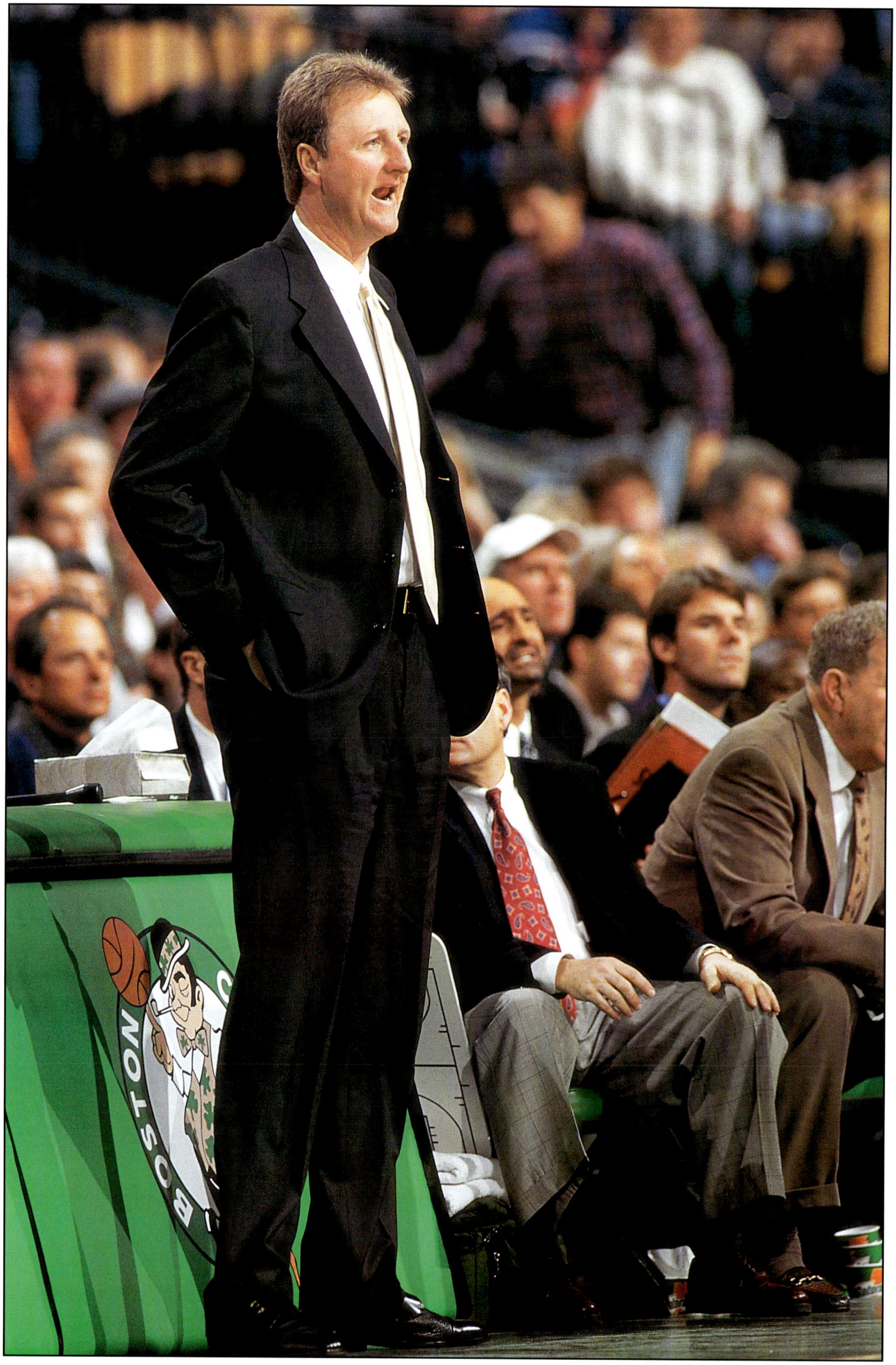
BOSTON

Indiana Gothic

Of Steve Lipofsky's many excellent photographs of Larry Bird, there is one, a portrait taken early in his career before Bird came to understand that he didn't have to stand around for photographers, that is my favorite. There's Bird, in blue jeans and boots and a green satin Celtics jacket, ball tucked under his arm and a thumb jammed in his pocket. This photograph so captures the essence of the young Larry that while looking at it you can almost hear the riffs of John Mellencamp's "I was born in a small town…"

It's pure Indiana gothic.

For nearly two decades now, Bird has been the proudest product of what is perhaps hoops' most intense subculture, Hoosier high school basketball. Yes, there have been the Rick Mounts, the Steve Alfords, the Damon Baileys, a select number of legendary hopefuls. There has even been the elite class, comprised of Oscar Robertson's and John Wooden's rare greatness.

Bird, though, resides alone at the top of the great hoops pyramid in Indiana, where basketball is worshipped with cultlike intensity.

And now Larry Bird has returned there. To coach the Indiana Pacers out of their doldrums. As a player, Bird never really inhabited the doldrums. If he wasn't injured, he was competing, burning actually, for the National Basketball Association title.

Somebody once asked him about a championship ring.

"I live for them things," Bird said.

As a coach, can he remanufacture that intensity he had as a player? That was the question that rolled across the minds of Indiana basketball fans in the late spring and early summer of 1997 as it became apparent that Bird would indeed take the job running the Pacers.

To those who knew Larry, those who had been his teammates, the answer was simple: If success depended on hard work and preparation, then Larry would master it. As a player, Larry had always been defined by unparalleled effort.

Like millions of other Bird fans, it was this effort that drew my admiration. As much as I treasure my memories of sitting on press row under the basket in Boston Garden and watching him ring up 20 points in a quarter in an awe-inspiring scoring display, those aren't my favorite Bird moments. When I think of Larry's greatness, I remember his pregame shootarounds in the dim emptiness of the Garden.

On most game nights, Bird would emerge from the locker room shortly before 6 p.m., well before other players took the floor. Except for the ushers lounging in the seats, a few media people preparing for the game and a respectful spectator or two, Bird usually had the floor to himself. Those times, more than any, the Garden fulfilled its reputation as a basketball temple, with the Celtics' umpteen championship banners hanging in the rafters and the ball echoing off the chipped and aged parquet floor. A pale, expressionless figure in green sweat

The Hick From French Lick.

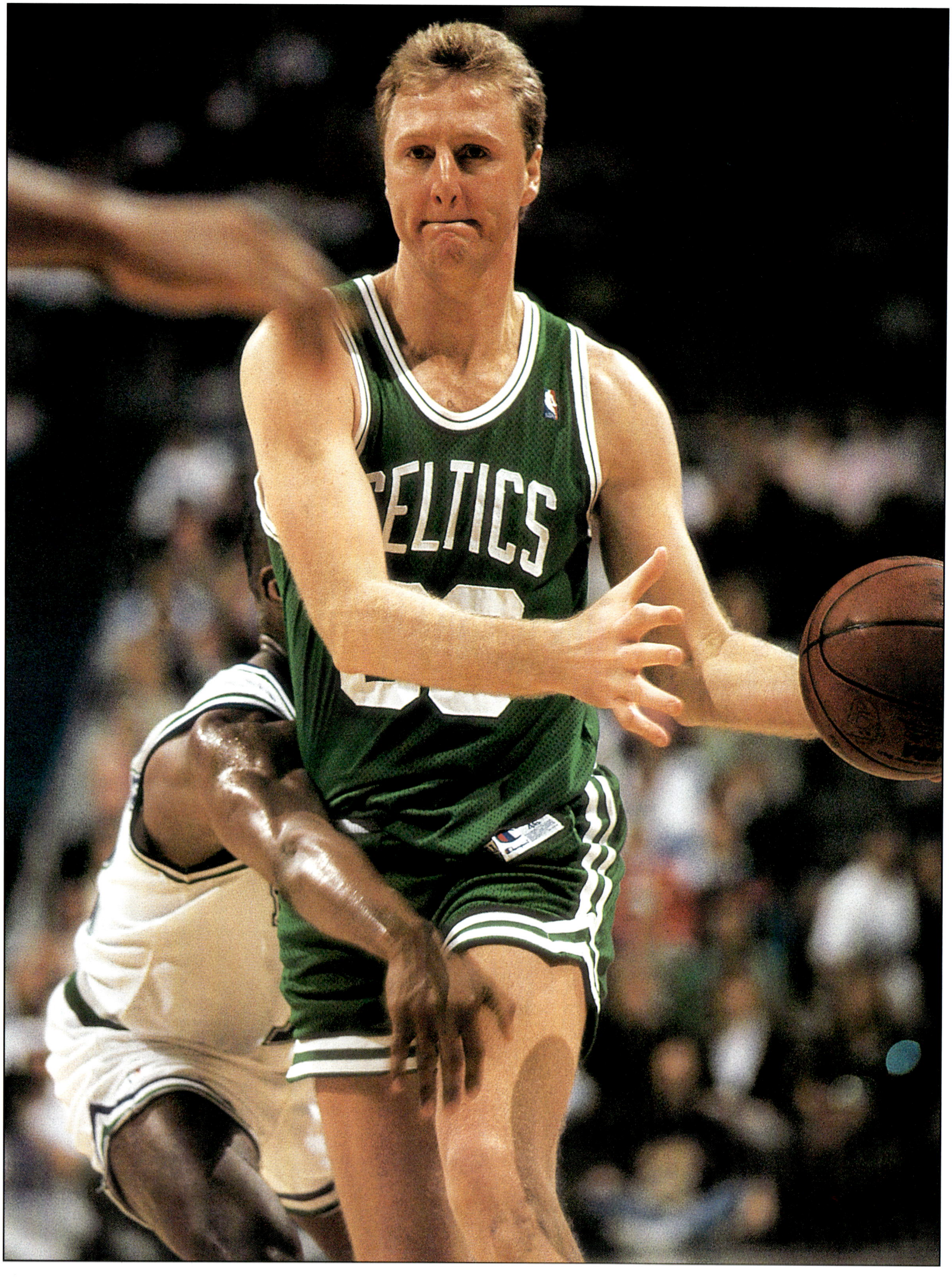
ELTICS

BIRD: Portrait of a Competitor

pants and a gray top, Bird was appropriately solemn for these occasions, as if he was intent on communing with the Great Roundball Spirits.

He usually began his shooting routine with free throws, six to 10 of them. He worked with Joe Qatato, the Celtics' assistant equipment manager, who would dutifully retrieve the ball after each shot and whip an efficient return pass. Bird would then shift into a shooting pattern with no exact routine, only his concentration to bind the sequence. Moving steadily, not quickly, Bird would sweat easily and wipe his brow at an occasional miss.

Some nights he would loft a few warmups, then head to the perimeter, moving left along the three-point arc toward the corner, taking each pass from Joe and converting it into a seemingly effortless jumper. From there, he would move to the paint and slough up soft left hooks. The left hook was obviously an acquired shot for Bird. He had to shepherd the ball into the basket. But the repetition of it in practice had allowed him to eliminate the natural hesitation in shooting it. Although a bit mechanical, the left hook was as neatly efficient a weapon as the rest of his repertoire.

From the low post Bird would circle right of the key for another series, then to the line for six to 10 more free throws. He would step back from the line after each hit, then move back into position and do it again until he was satisfied with the results. He would then shift to the top of the key for a series of half-set shots, half-jumpers, the muscles in his legs flexing enough to launch the ball, but not quite enough to lift him beyond gravity. He would strike repeatedly, each hit ripping the nets softly, rythmically. Bird's shot was a study in the conservation of effort. He would bring the ball up from the waist just to the right of his face, cocking it beside his right temple and releasing. The follow-through of his right hand and wrist would be bent fundamentally, holding until just before the ball reached its moment of swish.

At some point in the barrage, his confidence would click, prompting him to move again, this time left to the corner just inside the three-point line, where he would run up a dozen or more, as fast as Joe could send him the ball. From there, he would head to the low post and Joe would move to the perimeter to feed the ball down to him. Because he never shot it much as a youngster, Bird usually eschewed the bank shot, lofting the ball instead directly at the hoop.

Marveling at each of these shots were the select few Bird watchers who had found a way to slip into a courtside seat. For years, a regular spectator at these pre-game sessions was Carmen Rodriguez, a lawyer. In addition to a degree from the New England School of Law, she held a master's degree in the arts from the University of Madrid. Usually, Ms. Rodriquez spent much of her free time at the opera and the symphony, and she held season tickets to the ballet. Although she had no basketball background, Ms. Rodriguez became intrigued by Bird a few seasons

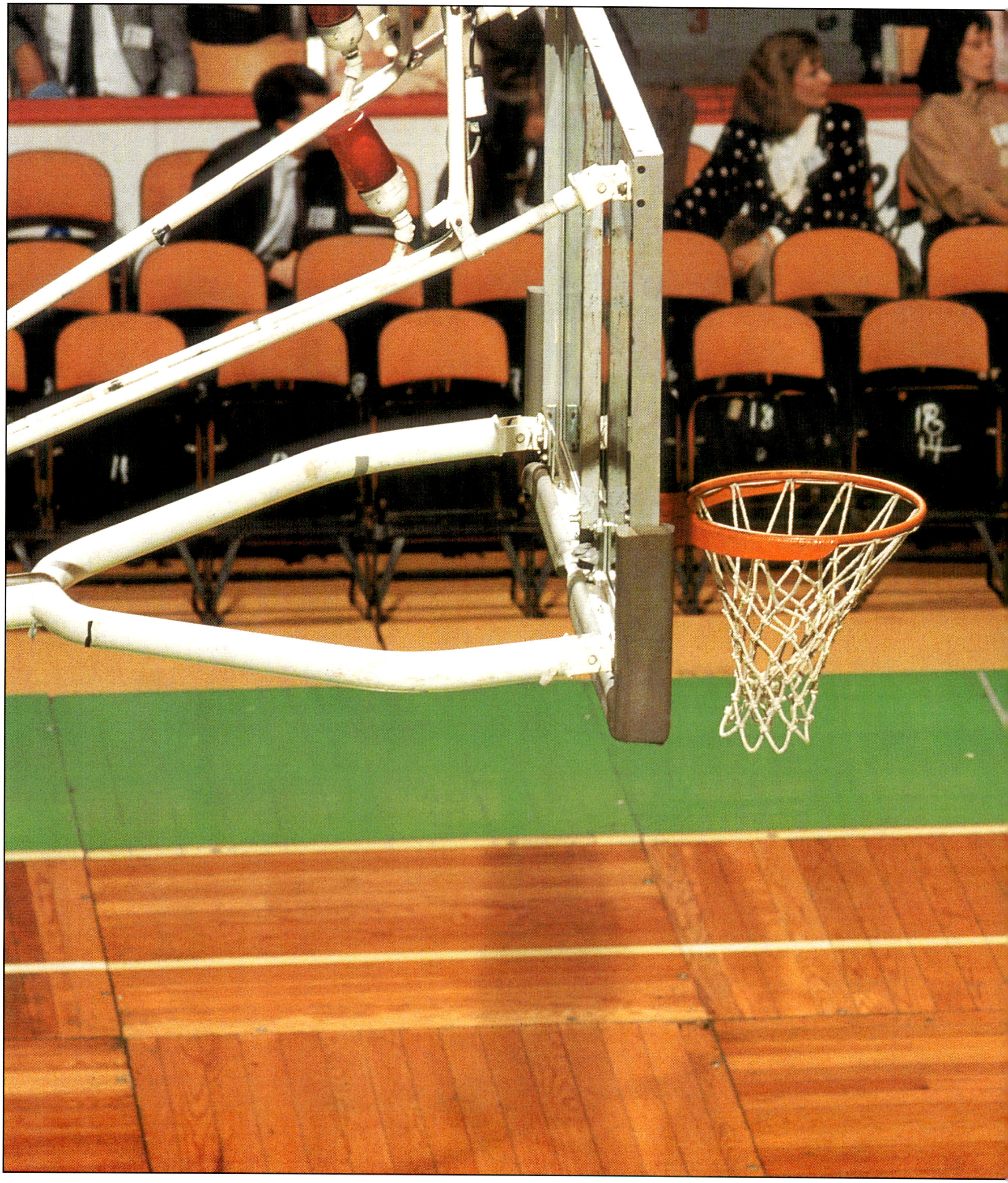

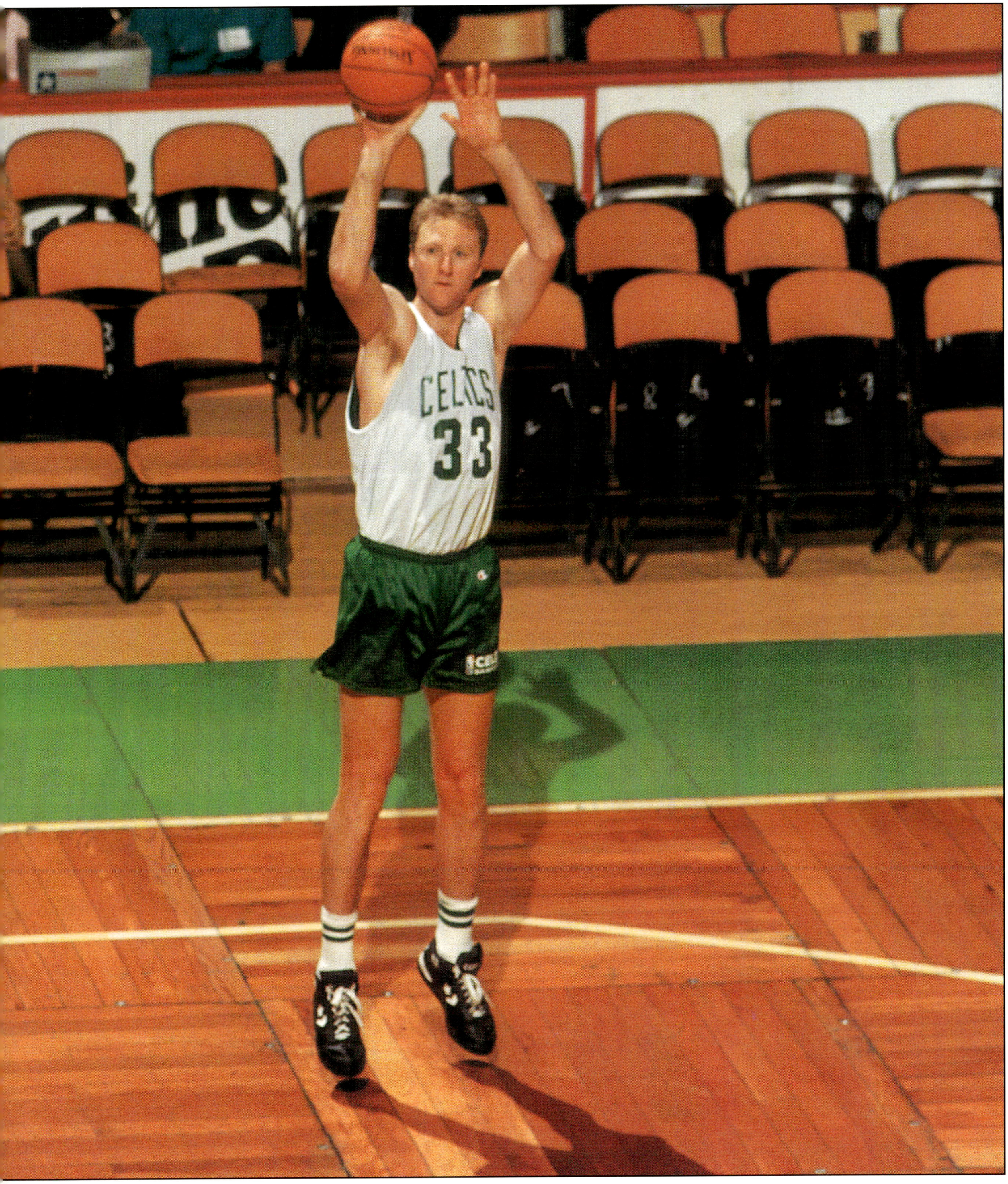
33

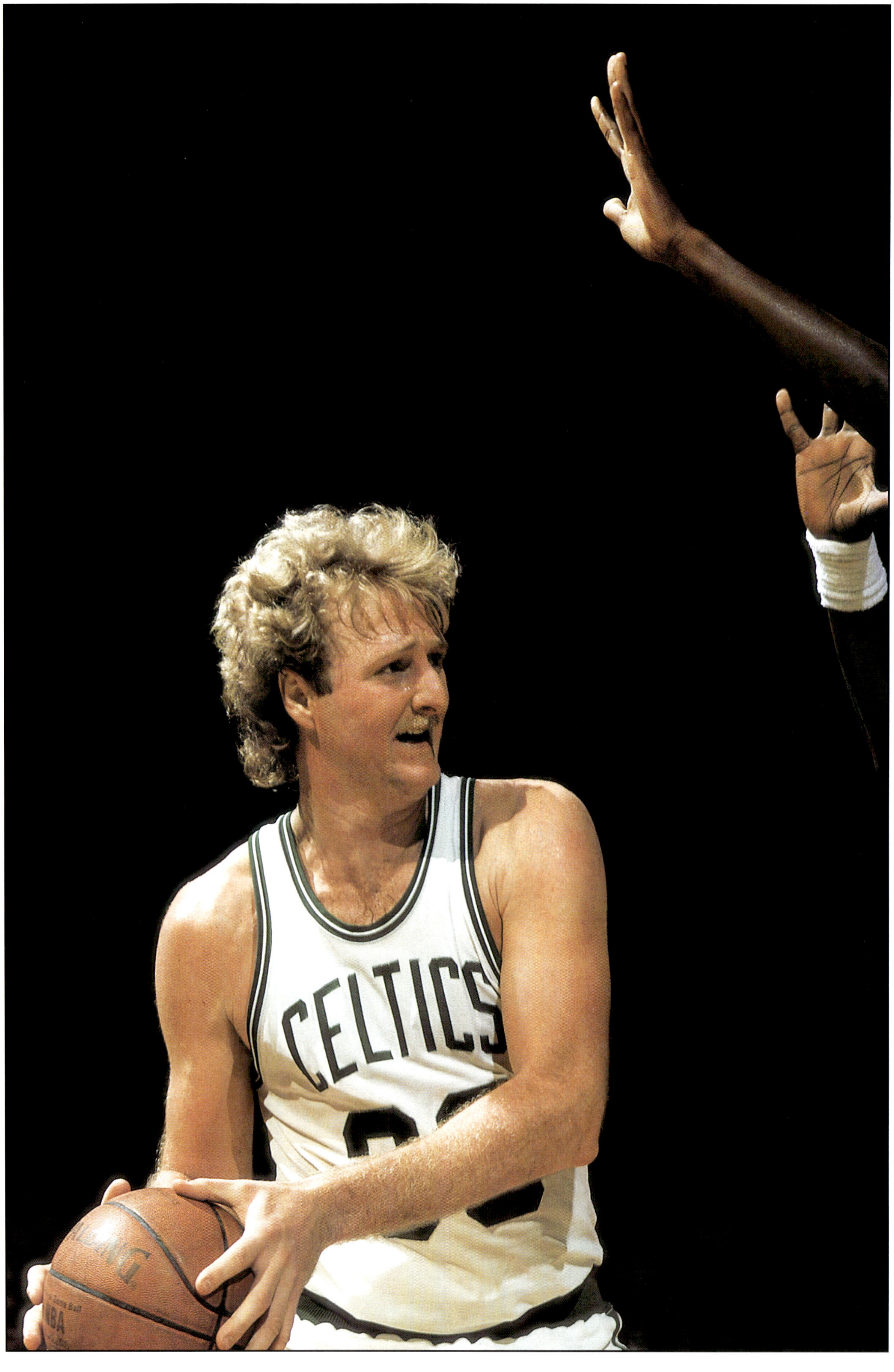
CELTICS

Indiana Gothic

after he arrived in Boston. Very soon, watching Boston's star had become her passion, a new twist in her appreciation of the arts.

"I think he's very smooth," she explained one night. "I think when he tosses the ball there's a finesse to it. His wrist, I think, is perfect. You've got to watch his wrist. And then watch his feet. But watch that wrist. It's beautiful. And his faces. I really believe he's a work of art. I don't need pictures of him. One of the press photographers offered a picture, and I said I didn't need it."

Ms. Rodriguez's favorite moments would come on nights when Bird was shooting well and his pace would mysteriously pick up. "That's the time I love the best," she explained. "He'll start to run around, and Joe will throw the ball and he runs from one end to the other. Then there are the times he's like a robot. He comes out and goes from here to here to there to do his routine. It's amazing. It's work. But that's what makes him great. It's work. Later on, you'll see the other guys come out to warm up… They're playing. But this guy doesn't screw around."

Joe, a goateed disciple, considered this practice time with Bird a special privilege. The sessions were work for Bird, and Qatato treated them the same. Sometimes they would fantasize game sequences together, Qatato explained, but that depended on Bird's mood. From working with Bird for years, Qatato had learned to sense Larry's mind and knew when he wanted to work in silence.

On a good night, Bird would shoot about 300 shots, sometimes more, making better than 80 percent of them. The intent was to work at every spot on the floor. Asked about his routine, Bird once said simply, "I don't count my shots. I just shoot 'til I feel good." Usually the conclusion to the session would be signalled by the stain of sweat soaking through the back of his shirt between the shoulder blades. Bird was always cautious not to work too much, although for the vast majority of NBA players, the idea of taking 300 shots before a game seemed almost insane.

"You can definitely leave your shot on the floor if you're not careful," Bird agreed.

It was this work ethic that propelled the Celtics to three world championships (1981, '84 and '86) over Bird's 13-year playing career. In getting those three championships and making a serious run at two others, Larry Legend led Boston to nearly 800 wins, eight divisional titles, and five conference crowns. As Celtics President Red Auerbach once explained, Bird was the driving force in Boston's success simply because he was the most motivated player

"The number one thing is desire," Larry once explained of his approach to the game, "the ability to do the things you have to do to become a basketball player. I don't think you can teach anyone desire. I think it's a gift. I don't know why I have it, but I do."

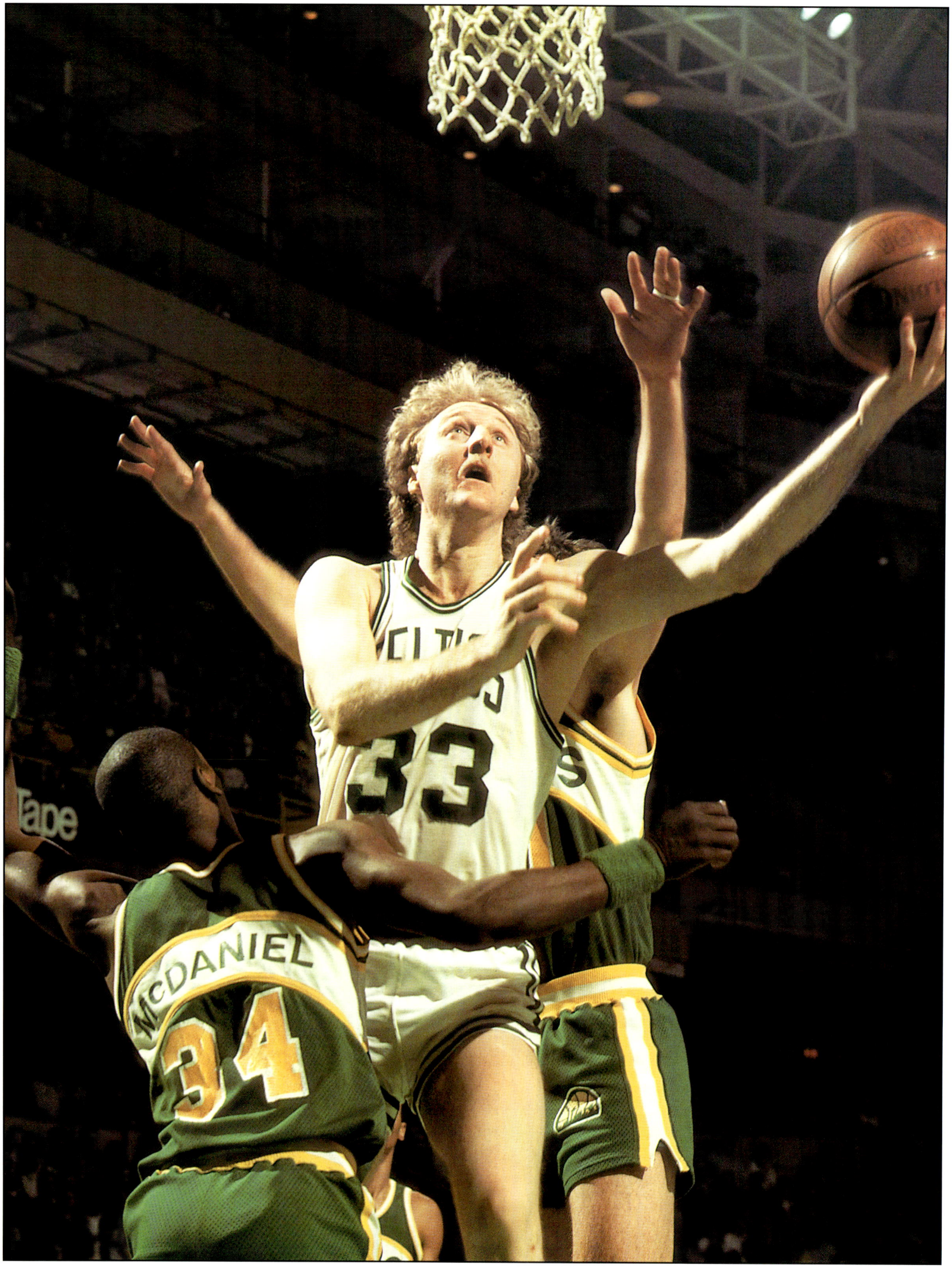
Tape
33
McDANIEL
34

Indiana Gothic

in the history of the game.

He worked endlessly to refine his skills. How fitting that Bird titled his 1990 memoir *Drive*. "The number one thing is desire," Larry once explained of his approach to the game, "the ability to do the things you have to do to become a basketball player. I don't think you can teach anyone desire. I think it's a gift. I don't know why I have it, but I do."

Asked to elaborate on Bird's place in the history of the game, Auerbach once told me, "There've been a lot of players over the years that have made a real impact on the game. Hank Luisetti's popularization of the one-handed shot. George Mikan with the hook shot. Sam Jones with bank shot. Wilt Chamberlain with the dunk and the power. Russell, who made the blocked shot an art. You can go right down the line. Larry Bird has made no singular contribution that has been revolutionary. All he does is teach what the effects of hard work and self-motivation can accomplish, and he refined his skills to the point where they were exceptional. Larry Bird will go down in history as one of the greatest that ever played the game. Larry Bird was not involved in any singular contribution. Neither was Magic Johnson, neither is Kareem Abdul-Jabbar. The same is true of Bob Cousy or Jerry West or Oscar Robertson or Dr. J., who were great players. They didn't make singular revolutionary contributions to the game. Even Michael Jordan hasn't.

"Larry has been very charismatic coming from the small town, Auerbach added, the little ol' country boy from French Lick, Indiana, and so forth. In reality he's very bright and he has great habits and he sets all these goals. You see, a lot of guys forget the Oscar Robertsons and the Cousys and the Dr. Js and so forth. But they were more of city type players, and it was an urban game originally. Whereas Larry Bird came out of a small town, small school that was not one of the top basketball programs. It's the Horatio Alger type of thing of a small town boy making good. That's why he captured the imagination of the people of the country, and that's why his contribution, I think, will never be forgotten."

> **"Larry has been very charismatic coming from the small town, the little ol' country boy from French Lick, Indiana, and so forth. In reality he's very bright and he has great habits and he sets all these goals. ... That's why he captured the imagination of the people of the country and that's why his contribution I think will never be forgotten."**
>
> **– Red Auerbach**

During his playing days, the perspectives around the NBA varied on the exact nature of Bird's greatness, but the high regard was almost universal. Longtime NBA player and coach Gene Shue called him the best forward ever. "There will be no one to compare with Oscar Robertson and Jerry West at guard and Bird at forward," Shue said. Pete Newell, one of the game's great minds, offered similar endorsements. Fellow players did, too. After Bird obliterated the Houston Rockets in the 1986 NBA Finals, Hakeem Olajuwon was left awestruck. "He's the greatest player I've ever seen," the Houston center told reporters.

On the subject of the greatest player, Bird was predictably circumspect during his career. "All I know," he says, "is that people tend to forget how great the older great players were. It'll happen that way with me, too."

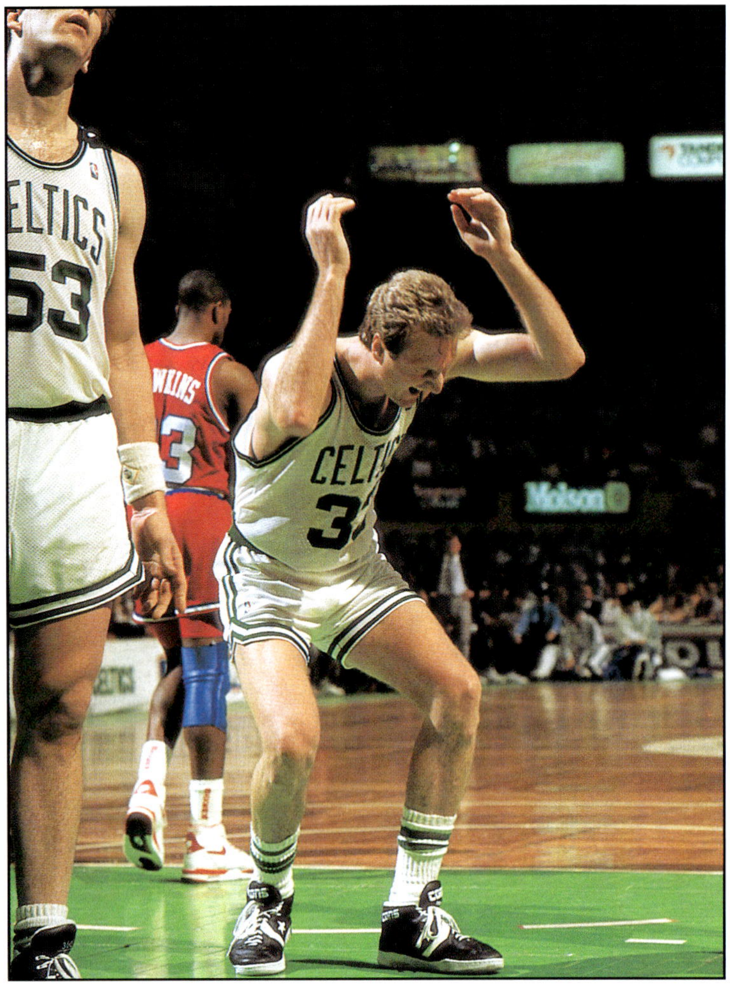
CELTICS
53
Molson

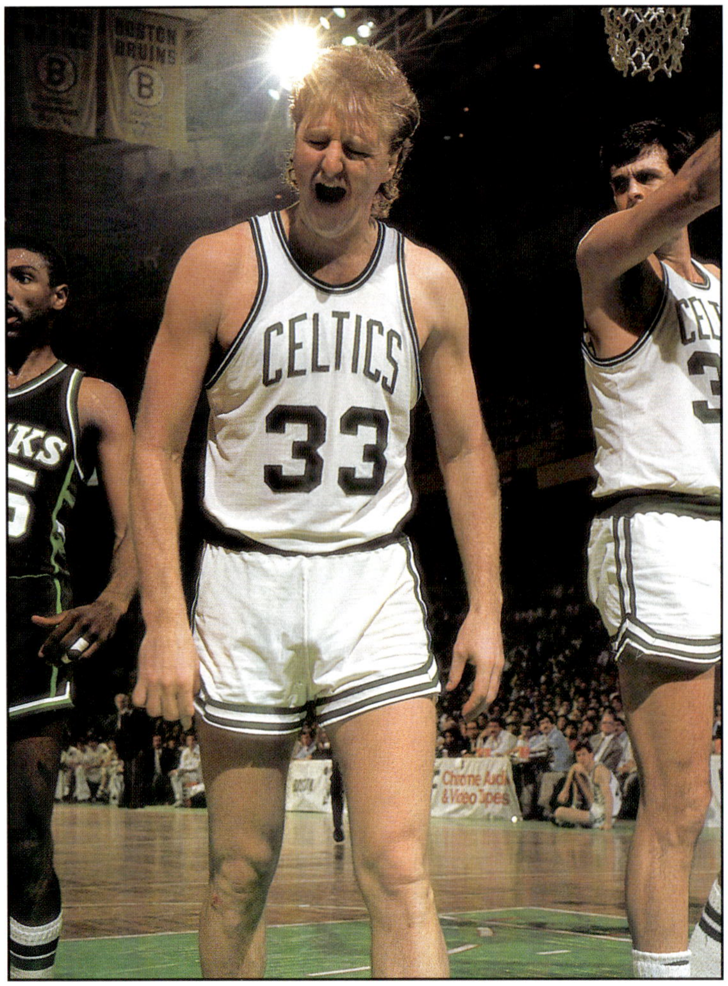
BOSTON BRUINS
CELTICS
33

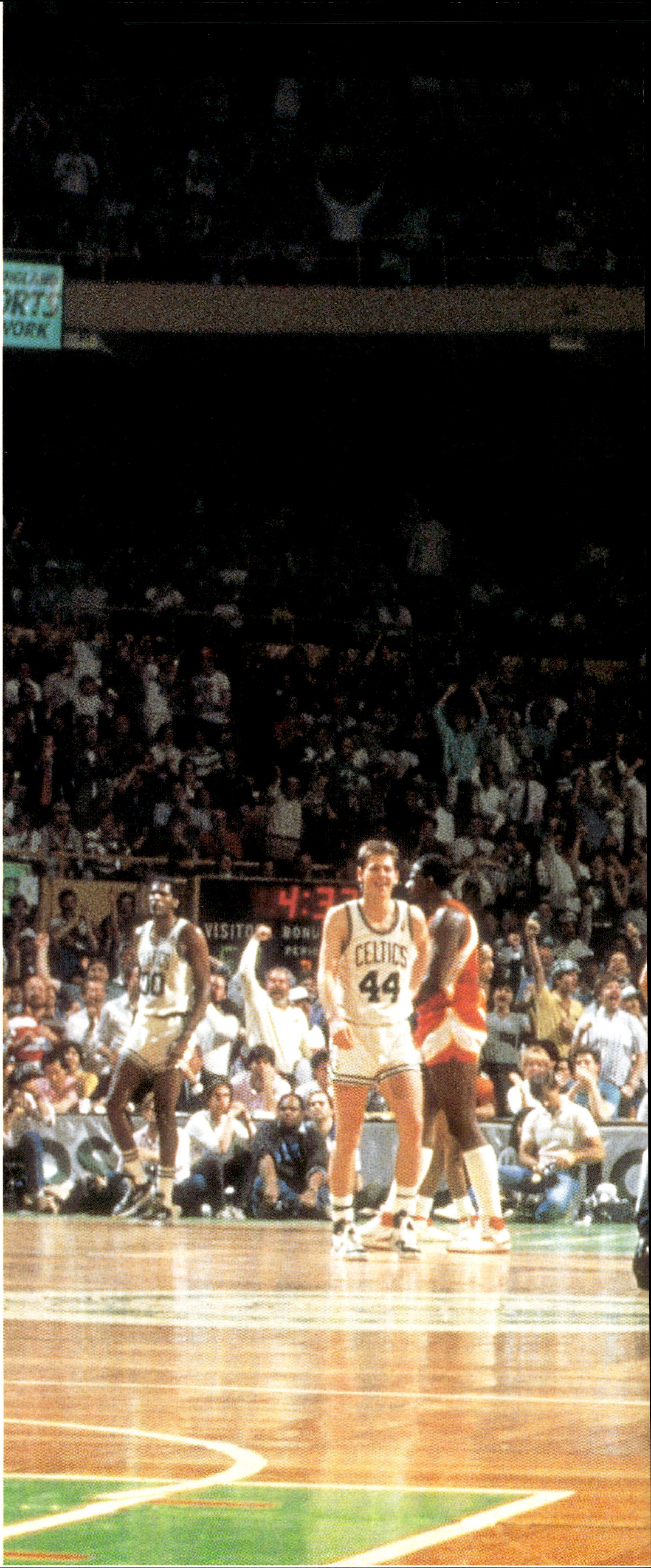
CELTICS
44

BOSTON BRUINS SPORTS SHOP
PARQUET PICASSO
BUSCH
24
JOHNSON
3
CELTICS
33
42
30
CELTICS

Indiana Gothic

Sweet Bird of Youth

Bird's shyness was as remarkable as his shooting when he first came to the attention of the national basketball scene as a junior at Indiana State in 1978. The fifth of six children, he was raised in a family that struggled to pay the bills in French Lick, a rural community of 2,265 in southwestern Indiana. His father, Joe, was a skilled laborer plagued by alcohol and debt. His mother, Georgia, worked as a waitress to keep her six kids going in the right direction. Bird has said the near poverty of his upbringing remains a large factor in his motivation. It is also the foundation of his work ethic and solid value system.

As a star at Springs Valley High, where his older brother had starred before him, Bird attracted the attention of college recruiters and eventually agreed to play for Bob Knight at Indiana University. But the campus at Bloomington, with its moneyed, well-dressed students, was worlds beyond Bird's experience. Within weeks, he decided to leave. "I'd just turned 17 and was away from home for the first time in my life," he explained later. "I wanted to go back home. I didn't tell nobody I was leaving. I just up and left on a Friday afternoon. I walked down to the interstate and thumbed a ride home to French Lick. I got home and told my mom, 'Ma, that place ain't for me.'"

Back home, he found work on a municipal maintenance crew that included part-time duty on a garbage truck. It was a fulfilling job nonetheless, affording him the opportunity to feel good about fixing up and cleaning up the community. Not long after his return, his father committed suicide. In a whirlwind, Bird married, fathered a daughter, Corrie, and divorced, all by age 19. In the midst of this turmoil, he returned to school at the less-imposing Indiana State in Terra Haute, a place where his game could find its own speed. There, after his sophomore year, he became friends with Max Gibson, a man in the coal business and a backer of Indiana State basketball. In the summer, Gibson gave Bird a job in maintenance. "He showed up and done his job every day, as you might guess," Gibson would later tell reporters. "Anything he started, he completed. I had a lot of ball players who had problems getting to work, but Larry was obviously different. You knew he'd be to work by 8 o'clock every morning."

By his senior year at Indiana State, he had found a new level of success, leading the Sycamores to the NCAA championship game against Michigan State and Magic Johnson. The country had become enamored of Bird's leadership of a small, unheralded team. His first major questioner was Billy Packer, then the college basketball analyst at NBC Sports, who made the regrettable midseason comment that Bird was overrated. Unused to the publicity and criticism, Bird was sheltered from the media by Coach Bill Hodges and the Indiana State staff. With his shyness, he projected to the college basketball audience a silent and sullen image, which contrasted greatly with the free-wheeling and talkative Magic Johnson. At the NCAA finals in Salt Lake City, Bird loosened up a bit. "To me, it's a serious game," he said when asked by reporters about the difference. "Now you wouldn't expect me to be havin' all kinds of fun when the score's tied, two seconds are left on the clock and the other guys have the ball. It's nice that Magic laughs a lot. I just hope he won't be laughing in my face after he makes a big play." Later, when Packer walked onto the floor before the title game, Bird orchestrated a gag where all the Indiana State players bombarded the broadcaster with practice balls.

Touted by Michigan State Coach Jud Heathcote as the meeting of the "Bird Man and Magic Man," the championship earned the highest television rating of any college basketball game ever, as a massive audience tuned

22

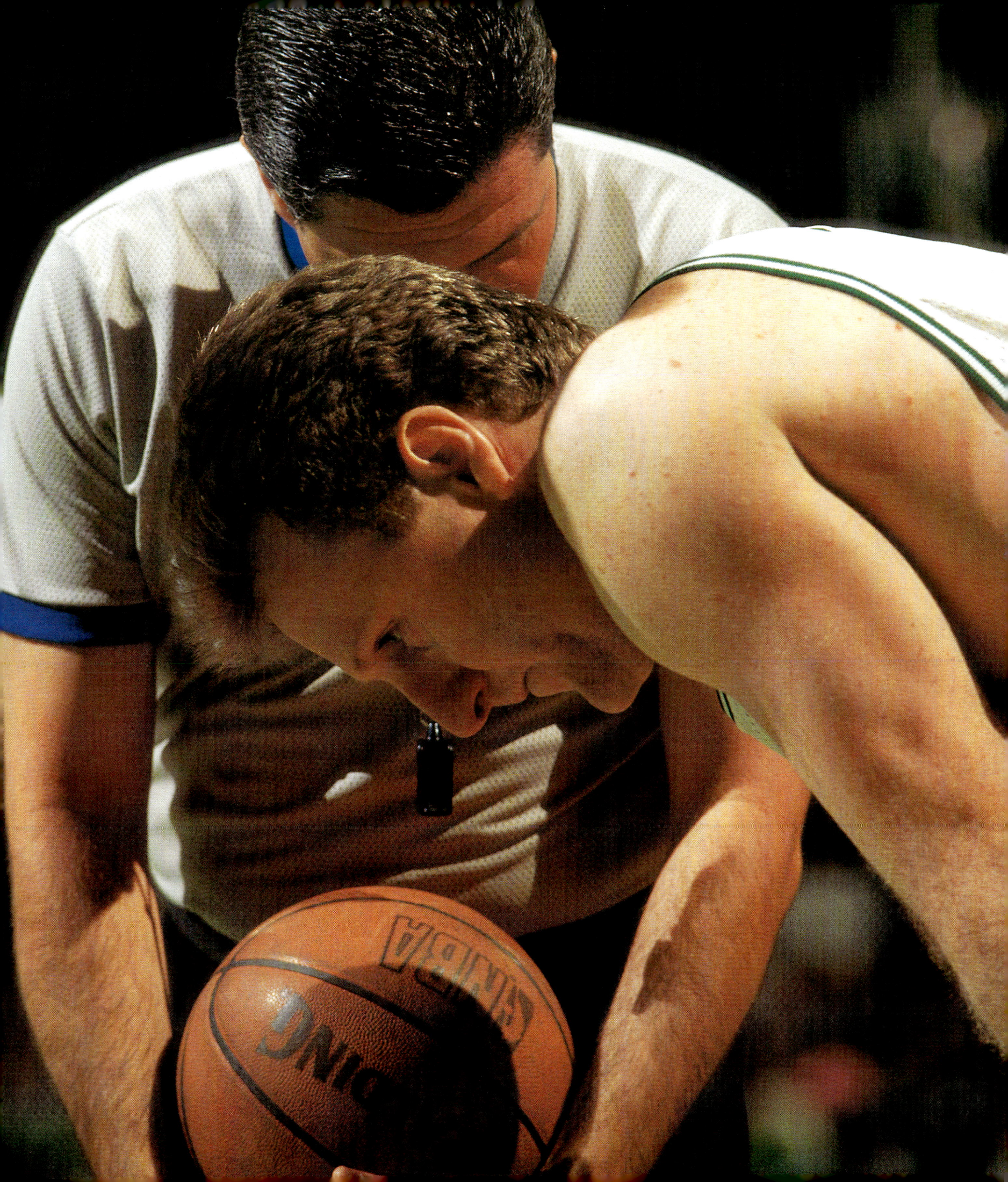
NBA

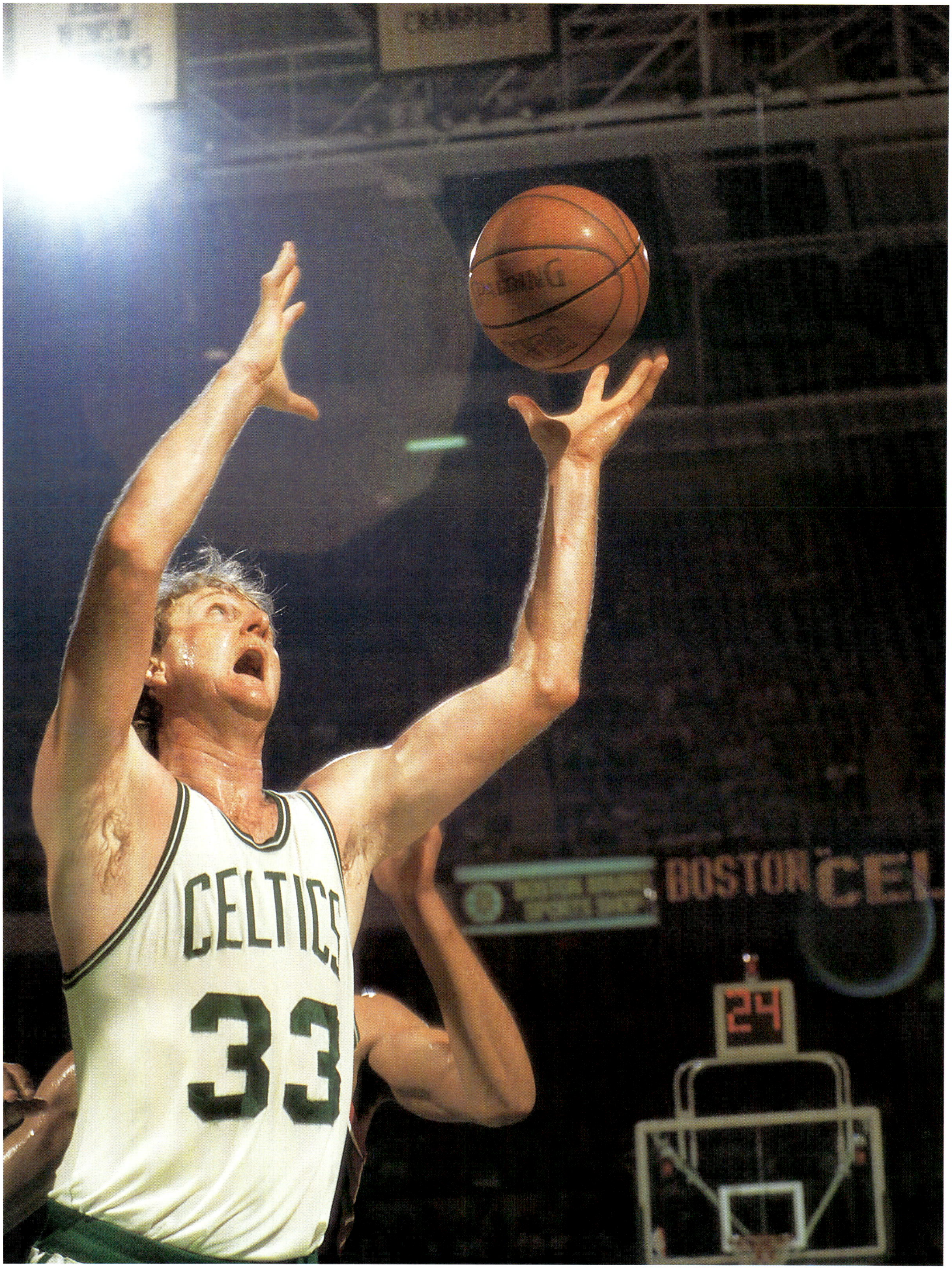
CHAMPIONS
CELTICS
33
BOSTON
CEL
24

Indiana Gothic

in and showed its sixth sense for history. Bird played with a broken thumb, and Michigan State took the title. But the destinies of the two players were inextricably linked. It's no secret that they didn't care for each other much in those early years of their careers. But their competition, their ability, and their endorsement contracts with Converse sneakers warmed their relations over the seasons into a solid friendship. "We're both the same," Johnson has said. "We'll do anything to win. You can list all the great players you want, but there are only a couple of winners."

"Whatever they have seems to rub off," K.C. Jones observed. "Russell had it, and I see the same thing in Larry and Magic."

Auerbach had drafted Bird with the sixth pick of the first round the previous spring (1978), leaving the Celtics a year to sign him. It was one of the all-time slick maneuvers in NBA personnel management. As a fifth-year college player, Bird was eligible for the draft, and Boston was willing to wait a year for his services. Auerbach and Bob Woolf, Bird's agent, dickered over the contract until finally agreeing on a $650,000-per-year deal, then the largest rookie contract in league history.

Some observers thought the contract was a huge gamble because Bird was from little Indiana State and was considered slow and unable to jump. He even played that angle up a bit that fall of 1979. "I've never considered myself a super athlete," Bird said." I admit I'm not the quickest guy in the world. In fact, I'm slow. But I've always tried to make up for that in other ways. I block out and I follow up shots for rebounds. And if there's a loose ball on the floor, I'll be down there bumping heads."

Not long after coming to Boston in 1979, Bird was interviewed by *Globe* sportswriter Mike Madden. "I was at a playground," Bird said, "and a little girl came up and asked me if I'd mind saying hello to her brother. She took me over to him. He was sitting in a wheelchair, retarded and badly crippled, and he couldn't really talk. He mostly made sounds. But I could hear him saying, 'Larry Bird. Larry Bird.' He started to reach out for me, and I grabbed him and held him in my arms. Then he mumbled something to his mother, and she nodded and told me he said he wanted to play basketball like I did. I've never been touched so deeply. I felt hurt all over and didn't know what to say, but something inside me was telling me to give that little boy something, so I just hugged him and told him I really hoped that it would be possible someday.

"You know," Bird told Madden, "it's the kids who I'd really like to do something for, especially kids who don't always have it so good. Whenever I go to a school or clinic, I always look for the kid who doesn't have the nicest clothes, or who looks like he doesn't have very many nice things. Those are the kids I try to spend my time with, because I identify with them. That's how I came up."

> "We're both the same," Johnson has said. "We'll do anything to win. You can list all the great players you want, but there are only a couple of winners."

BIRD: Portrait of a Competitor

The Confidence Game

Diversity is what made Bird's game so special. The one move that came closest to emerging as his signature was the step back, a moving away from the defender to create shooting or driving room. Yet he was just as well-known for his developed ambidexterity and his passing style. Prominent in his portfolio was a capacity for making freakish plays seem common.

He produced them almost nightly, giving the definite impression that perhaps he had an ethereal horse shoe in his back pocket. His brilliant fourth quarter against the Atlanta Hawks in Game 7 of the 1988 Eastern Conference semifinals contained a memorable sequence: Driving against Cliff Levingston, Bird stumbled in the lane, was fouled, fell forward until almost parallel with the floor, and as the 24-second clock expired, pitched up a blind left-handed hook that banked neatly in. He rose after the ball fell through, then wiped his face, adjusted his shirt and sank the free throw, all critical in getting the Celtics the win. He produced so many similarly unbelievable shots and passes over the years, Boston Garden fans became more than a bit spoiled by an overdose of the supernatural.

Despite his often-mentioned lack of leaping ability, Bird's positioning, timing and strong hands made him an ideal rebounder. And his offense had a hauteur to it, particularly when he could make a play at a crucial moment that killed the spirit of an opponent. His favorite weapon in those situations was the three-point shot. Bob Ryan of the *Boston Globe*, a legendary Bird watcher, was fascinated by the fact that, while Bird was philosophically opposed to the three-pointer, he used it time and again with devastating accuracy. Bird based his opposition on a belief that the three-pointer shouldn't alter the outcome of a game. He also thought officials had too much difficulty ascertaining whether a player's feet were in position behind the line. His philosophical ponderings, however, didn't prevent him from annually blowing by the opposition in the NBA's three-point shootout during the All-Star Game. He won the shootout the first three years of its existence. When the NBA began its long-range competition in 1986, he entered the locker room before the shootout and asked his fellow contestants, "All right, who's playing for second?"

That competitiveness was his essence, and it didn't matter whether the circumstances were an NBA Finals game or a mere ho-hum drill in practice. During the 1988 playoffs, the Celtics broke into three-man teams for their routine shooting drill. With the first team to reach a point total declared winners, Bird's team hustled toward the final bucket tied with Artis Gilmore's team. He and Gilmore each had a final shot at the basket. Both had drawn back to shoot when Bird's hauteur took over. He held his shot to give the other team a chance, snickered when Gilmore missed, then calmly sank the winner.

"Anything Larry does, he tries to be the best at it," said his younger brother Eddie, who followed Larry at Indiana State. "He's always got to be first in anything that he does."

"I guess I try to carry myself in a certain way on the court," Bird once said of his hauteur. "It's funny because nobody else in my family is like that. It's not that I don't have respect for my opponents. When you lose that, you've got nothing. But tradition is important here, acting like a Celtic."

K.C. Jones, who coached the Celtics for five of Bird's nine seasons, saw proof of greatness many times over. "There's so many factors involved with him," Jones explained once after Bird had gone all-out during a preseason game. "People don't see everything he does. He's such a hard-nosed competitor and very determined. You don't see superstars like him going after loose balls —

22 14
23 15
21 25
24 6
BOSTON CELTICS
1981 WORLD CHAMPIONS
BOSTON CELTICS
1976 WORLD CHAMPIONS
BOSTON CELTICS
CELTICS

especially in pre-season games. His effort is always there."

The other major bauble in Bird's collection was his confidence. Every time he took a shot, he believed it was going in. At times in his career, his self-assurance would shine so brightly that it fused his game at a higher level, fortifying his teammates, blinding his opponents and mesmerizing just about everyone else involved. "I just felt there was no one in the league who could stop me if I was playing hard," he said in accepting his 1986 MVP award. "What makes me tough to guard is that once I'm near the three-point line, I can score from anywhere on the court. It's kind of hard to stop a guy who has unlimited range."

His confidence was an integral part of the Celtics' team psyche, as well. "When I score points and I'm on, everbody's on," Bird once explained. "If I'm playing well, everyone plays well. They look at me and they think, 'Well, he can score any time for us,' and it loosens them up. It's a great feeling to be in."

Bird, however, was also the first to acknowledge that such confidence had a double edge, particularly in the extra pressure it carried. When he wasn't shooting well, his downturn could have a disastrous effect on team confidence. Regardless, he was virtually unflappable.

"If it don't go down, it don't go down," he used to say. "I don't worry about it. To tell you the truth, I go out there and give it my best. If it's not good enough, I try to come back the next game and have a better game. There's no use in me worrying about my shooting because I'm not going to change anything and I'm going to keep practicing on it. If it goes in, it goes in. It's been awful good to me over the years, and there's no use panicking because it's not going in for three games."

Even during his slumps, Bird could use his rebounding, passing and other skills to control the outcome. Of these "other" skills at Bird's disposal, it was his passing that set him apart from other forwards. In the negotiations for Bird's rookie contract, his agent, the late Bob Woolf, argued that as a dominant player Bird was worth $1 million per year. Auerbach attempted to counter that centers, occasionally guards, dominated NBA play, but never forwards, never from the corner of the floor. But over the course of his career, Bird proved that his passing demoralized opponents almost as much as his three-point shot. "I grew up all of a sudden," he once said of his adolescence. "I was a guard as a sophomore and junior in high school, before I grew up. And we had some great shooters. I tried to get the ball to the great shooters. Passing is so much a part of basketball, it's unbelievable. It don't matter who scores the points. It's who gets the ball to the scorer."

Bird prized this code of "team first" his entire career. "You can call any of my teammates right now," he would say a dozen years later, "and I guarantee you they'll tell you there never was a time when I wouldn't give them the ball if I saw them open. You've just got to work together."

Working together, to Bird, provided the opportunity to overcome his natural liabilities. "Guys who were quicker than me sometimes got around me on defense," he explained, "so I was looking for help a lot of the time. But no one minded, because every time one of my teammates got beaten that way, he knew for sure that he could count on me for the same kind of help."

By his own admission, Bird's lack of speed made him a question mark in the man-to-man defensive schemes of the NBA. Yet, he developed as an excellent "team defense" player, showing persistent off-ball effort, pulling in clusters of crafty steals and exhibiting such a penchant for hanging back in the lane that he prompted a redefining of the league's illegal defense rule. In his second, third and fourth seasons, he was named to the league's all-defensive second team, whose rosters were selected by the coaches.

The underlying element of his success as a player was a deep and abiding personal pride, which should serve him well as a coach. "I think that he is proud that he has a singular ability," observed Ryan, the collaborator on Bird's autobiography, "that of all the people in all the world, that this particular kid living in this particular depressed area of Indiana and being the wrong race in the wrong sport, that he has overcome those things. And he is proud, I believe, that he has done it by working and by dedication."

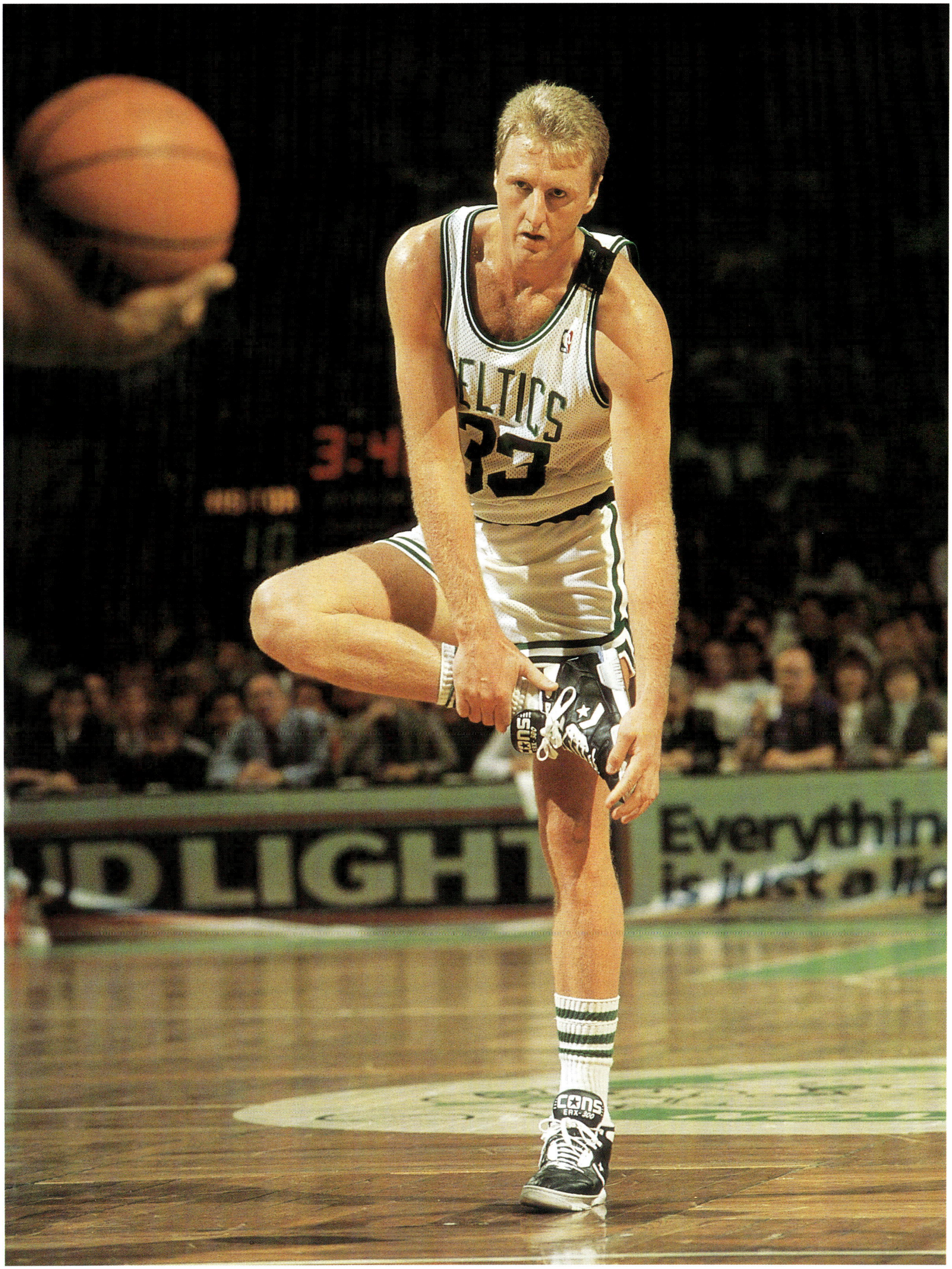
CELTICS
33
3:4
DLIGHT
Everythin
CONS
ERX-300

Each night during introductions, Larry would gaze into the Garden rafters and fix his concentration on the banner honoring Boston Bruin Bobby Orr, Bird's private symbol of excellence.

Garden Glory

Larry Bird's first real NBA test came in Boston's opening 1979-80 exhibition game with the Philadelphia 76ers and Julius Erving. Shooting seven of 15 from the field, Bird scored 18 points, but the 'Sixers won easily, 115-90. "I guess the best thing to say is that he can play," Erving commented afterward. "He's what he's supposed to be, what you've read about. You can feel the intensity he has, the moves. He can create his own offense; he was talking all the time out there. I have a very favorable opinion of him as a player."

Bird's presence had an immediate impact on a Celtic team that had gone 29-53 (the franchise's most losses in a season) in 1978-79. In its misery, the team had played before only one sold-out crowd at Boston Garden the entire season. Playing with Nate Archibald, Dave Cowens, Cedric Maxwell, Rick Robey, M.L. Carr and Chris Ford, Bird transformed Boston into a team that blazed through the 1979-80 season to a league-best 61-21 record. The Celtics fell 4-1 to Philadelphia in the conference finals, but the immediate reversal was enough to answer questions about Bird. He had averaged better than 21 points and 10 rebounds over the regular season and outpolled Magic in the league Rookie of the Year voting. As might be expected, an empty seat in the Garden became a thing of the past.

Cowens retired for 1980-81 and was replaced in the lineup by Robert Parish, who had been acquired from Golden State. The other big Celtic addition was the drafting of Kevin McHale. In the backcourt, Chris Ford started alongside the 6'1" Archibald. The league had just installed its three-point shot in 1979, and Ford quickly acquired the distinction of making the first trey in league history.

A New Yorker, Archibald's instincts had been honed on a Bronx playground. Then he attended Texas-El Paso, and afterword was drafted by the Kansas City Kings, where he was groomed and coached by Bob Cousy. He adopted much of the former Boston great's freewheeling approach to the game. In 1972-73, Archibald had led the league in scoring (34 points per game) and assists (11 per game). But in Boston, his scoring wasn't as important as his play-making. He had a knack for distributing the ball just where Bird wanted it.

"There is nobody better than Tiny," Larry declared.

For Boston coach Bill Fitch, the basketball ideal was a motion offense that wound its way toward an inside bucket. He stressed passing and disciplined patterns of play. Having been an excellent college coach at North Dakota, he liked hard workers who accepted their roles. Which is exactly how Ford and backup point guard Gerald Henderson approached the game. And M.L. Carr was another in the same mold.

The frontcourt had the makings of greatness. Maxwell was at the height of his career, and McHale quickly showed an ability to score and block shots. Plus he was happy to come off the bench. Parish, too, played

BIRD: Portrait of a Competitor

with pride and grace. He ran the floor and shot his startlingly accurate rainbow jumper, which he had acquired in high school in Shreveport, Louisiana, when his coach made him shoot over an extended broom.

Out of the gate, this group struggled to a 7-5 record, and Bird placed the blame on himself. "Max isn't scoring enough," he said, "and it's my fault, because I should be getting the ball to him. I know how to do it, and I haven't been doing it."

Like Magic with the Lakers, Bird's passing sustained the Celtics. He had to learn to keep his teammates involved. That facet of his game improved greatly as the season progressed, and the Celtics grew into an inspiring example of precise ball movement. From their fast breaks to their half-court game, they developed a knack for finding the open man.

Their competition again in the Eastern Conference was the Philadelphia 76ers, who had added an impressive rookie in guard Andrew Toney. The teams split their series, 3-3, but the tiebreaker gave Boston the home-court advantage in the playoffs.

After a first-round bye, Boston blew past Chicago in the second round, setting up another meeting with Philadelphia in the Eastern Finals. The Celtics felt confident and ready. Then like that, they lost their first game at home, captured the second and lost two more in Philadelphia. Suddenly, they had fallen behind, 3-1, and were facing a repeat of 1980, when the Sixers moved them aside, 4-1.

Facing the fifth game in Boston Garden, Fitch told his players he had been associated with only one team that had ever come back from a 3-1 deficit, but he felt this team could do it.

"I'm telling you, it was the most rewarding experience a group of guys can have in this sport," he said.

They responded by trailing 59-49 at halftime. In the locker room, Fitch made one more appeal, this time a shouting one. He said he didn't mind losing but he did mind seeing them play passively.

They worked hard over the next two quarters, but with 1:51 to go, the Sixers led by six and Boston's season seemed over. Then Maxwell blocked Andrew Toney's shot, and Archibald took the ball to the other end, where he scored and drew the foul for a three-point play. Like that, the lead was three, 109-106.

The Sixers tried to inbound the ball, but Boston's defense forced them to call two timeouts. When they did attempt to make the pass, Bird stole it and scored, cutting the lead to one. Then Boston's M. L. Carr got another steal and drew a foul. He hit both shots to give Boston the lead, 110-109. Bobby Jones got a shot for Philly, but Parish hampered it. Carr rebounded and was fouled again, enabling Boston to survive, 111-109.

The Celtics, though, didn't have much reason to celebrate. They trailed 3-2 and were headed to the Spectrum for Game 6. Boston hadn't won in Philly in the 11 games they had played there during Bird's pro career.

Boston's failure seemed a sure bet in the first half, as the Sixers went up by 12. Then in the second half, Maxwell got involved in a brouhaha with the Philly fans under one of the baskets. The Boston bench came to his aid, and when order was restored, Maxwell went to work, scoring, and rebounding like a madman. Late in the game, Boston had the ball and the lead, 96-95, when Bird took a 20-footer as the shot clock ran down. The ball hit the rim, rose up and fell back through, 98-95. Toney raced back upcourt with the ball and shot in the lane, but McHale blocked it. Moments later, Maxwell would hit two free throws to keep Boston alive, 100-98.

Game 7 was another fight. Philly led by 11 late in the second half and was still up, 89-83, with 4:34 on the game clock. The Celtics fought back to tie it at 89, and seconds later Bird came up with a loose ball. He rushed upcourt, looked off to his right, then fired up an 18-foot bank shot. Good! That was momentum enough. Philly added a free throw, but Boston held on, 91-90, to seal another great comeback.

Larry drives on Philly's Bobby Jones.

The Eastern Conference showdown in the 1980s usually came down to Larry and the Celtics vs. Julius and the Sixers.

"There was no one else in the world I wanted to have the ball but me," Bird said later of his last shot. With it, he had sent his team to the Finals.

Out west, Magic and the Lakers had fallen on hard times. He had suffered a cartilage tear in his knee during the season, then struggled back from surgery to rejoin his team late in the schedule. But they never had time to jell. Instead, they lost to Moses Malone and a plodding Houston Rockets team, 2-1, in the opening round. Houston had finished a mediocre 40-42 in the regular season, after spending the year trying to be a running team. But a late-season loss to Boston convinced Coach Del Harris that he needed to slow the approach to Malone's pace. After dumping the Lakers, the Rockets whipped San Antonio and Kansas City to meet Boston for the championship.

The Rockets' backcourt featured Mike Dunleavy, Calvin Murphy and Allen Leavell. Robert Reid was a smooth swing player, while Rudy Tomjanovich and Billy Paultz helped Malone up front.

Garden Glory

Houston had lost the previous dozen games to the Celtics. But Malone, who averaged nearly 28 points and 15 rebounds, declared that the Celtics were chumps. Game 1 in Boston Garden was surprisingly tight. Houston led 57-51 at the half. Late in the fourth period, with Boston struggling, Bird came upcourt and put up an 18-footer from the right side. As soon as he let it go, he knew it was bad and rushed to the rebound. He caught the ball in mid-air as his momentum carried him past the baseline. In an instant, he switched to his left hand (a right-handed shot would have hit the side of the backboard) and swished a 12-footer. The crowd went nuts, with Auerbach leading the cheers. Bill Russell, who was broadcasting the game for CBS, looked on in disbelief. "Larry was able to make the play," Russell said, "because he not only knew where the ball was going to land—he knew that he knew."

The shot carried Boston to a 98-95 win and left Auerbach puffing another cigar. "It was the one best shot I've ever seen a player make," he said afterward.

Floor Burns. Bird often wound up on the parquet during the '81 season.

"Bird sort of flipped it," Houston's Robert Reid said. "What can you say about a play like that?"

After playing on emotion for four straight games, Boston came out flat for Game 2. Fitch was so infuriated he put his fist through a blackboard in the locker room at half-time. That did little good, though. Houston's precision and Malone's inside play and rebounding kept the game close. Then the Rockets stole it at the end, 91-90.

"Sometimes a slap in the face wakes you up," Carr said.

Duly awakened, the Celtics responded with a 94-71 blowout of the Rockets in the Summit. Maxwell did much of the work for Boston, as Reid held Bird to just eight points.

Harris used just six players in Game 4, and Houston again held Bird to eight. Malone ruled the inside, and Houston got a 91-86 win that evened the series at 2-all. Afterward, Malone told the writers he could get four guys off the streets of Petersburg, Virginia, his hometown, and beat the Celtics. "I don't think they're all that good," he said. "I don't think they can stop us from doing what we want to do."

The Celtics vanquished Houston in the 1981 NBA Finals.

Garden Glory

Attracting a crowd against Philly.

It was just the emotional spark the Celtics needed. "The man threw down a challenge," Maxwell replied, "and this is a team that responds well to challenges."

With Maxwell leading, they took Game 5 in Boston, 109-80, for a 3-2 lead.

"The Celtics are still chumps," Malone said afterward.

The series returned to Houston that Thursday night, May 14, where Bird broke out of a slump. Boston had a six-point lead at the half and kept it down the stretch. When Houston pulled close late in the fourth, Bird came downcourt and canned his only three-pointer of the series, which sent Boston on to a 102-91 win and the team's 14th championship.

Afterward in the locker room, Bird stole Auerbach's lit cigar and puffed impishly.

"We're the champions," he said as he broke into a coughing spell.

"He's just one of a kind," Fitch said.

37

BIRD: Portrait of a Competitor

For four seasons, they had danced around each other in the NBA, meeting only twice each year in regular-season games. Still, Larry and Magic Johnson were always aware of each other. They searched the headlines and kept their eyes on the standings and the box scores. In a sense, their competition was reduced to the agate type on the inside sports pages. That, of course, was no way for two great players and two great teams to decide who was best. The Celtics and Lakers needed a showdown. The fans wanted it, the players wanted it, and finally it happened. Magic and the Lakers met Bird and the Celtics in the Finals. Across America, it was portrayed as a clash of symbols.

East vs. West. Tradition vs. New Wave. Hollywood vs. Beantown. Showtime vs. Shamrocks. Celtic Pride vs. L.A. Cool.

"It's like the opening of a great play," Lakers General Manager Jerry West told the writers just before the 1984 Finals. "Everyone's waiting to see it."

The media hype was tremendous. But beneath all the symbols and media, at the heart of everything, were two guys with immense confidence, supreme talent, and a mutual desire to dominate.

As Magic once explained, "I only know how to play two ways. That's reckless and abandon."

And that's how they approached their championship bash. Reckless and abandon. Two forces of pride and ego colliding. In retrospect, the league can be ever so thankful that they did. The Boston/Los Angeles fling in the Finals provided the juice for the NBA's resurgence. Over Larry and Magic's first dozen years in the league, television rights money alone zoomed from roughly $14 million per year to more than $100 million. "There's no question that Bird and Magic together, with the rivalry they brought us, was an important factor," Russ Granick, the NBA's executive vice president, said during the 1980s.

Things had gone awry for the Boston Celtics after their 1981 title. They kept adding quality players and kept looking better and better on paper. But on court they still lacked something. In the fall of 1981 they had obtained Danny Ainge, the former Brigham Young guard who had decided to play pro baseball with the Toronto Blue Jays. Boston had wrested Ainge away from the Blue Jays in a court battle. Then the Celtics had traded for backup point guard Quinn Buckner and a smooth-shooting former all-star forward, Scott Wedman. The only problem with these acquisitions was the ensuing traffic jam. Where and when would they all play? It wasn't an easy question to answer. When Milwaukee swept Boston in the 1983 playoffs, Red Auerbach decided it was time for yet more changes. Big ones.

Just weeks after the season ended, Bill Fitch resigned and was promptly replaced by assistant K.C. Jones. The two coaches had had their tiffs during Fitch's four-year tenure in Boston. Fitch's autocratic approach didn't allow much input from K.C., leaving the assistant openly frustrated at times. Jones approached the task of head coach from a completely different perspective than his predecessor. K.C. was a players' coach. He had been one of them. He understood them. He treated them as adults and welcomed their opinions, which wasn't Fitch's style. And where Fitch was a practice monster who spent hours reviewing videotape and expected his players to do the same, K.C. was a bit more laid back, a bit less insistent. Practices were important with Jones, but he favored a relaxed setting. Most of all, he wanted the complete effort from his players at game time, and as the record would reveal, he usually got it.

Auerbach made another big change heading into the 1983-84 season—the acquisition of guard Dennis Johnson from Phoenix for center Rick Robey. The Celtics needed a big defensive guard to match up against Sidney Moncrief in Milwaukee and Andrew Toney in Philadelphia, and the 6'4" Johnson fit just that bill. They also had Ainge, Buckner and

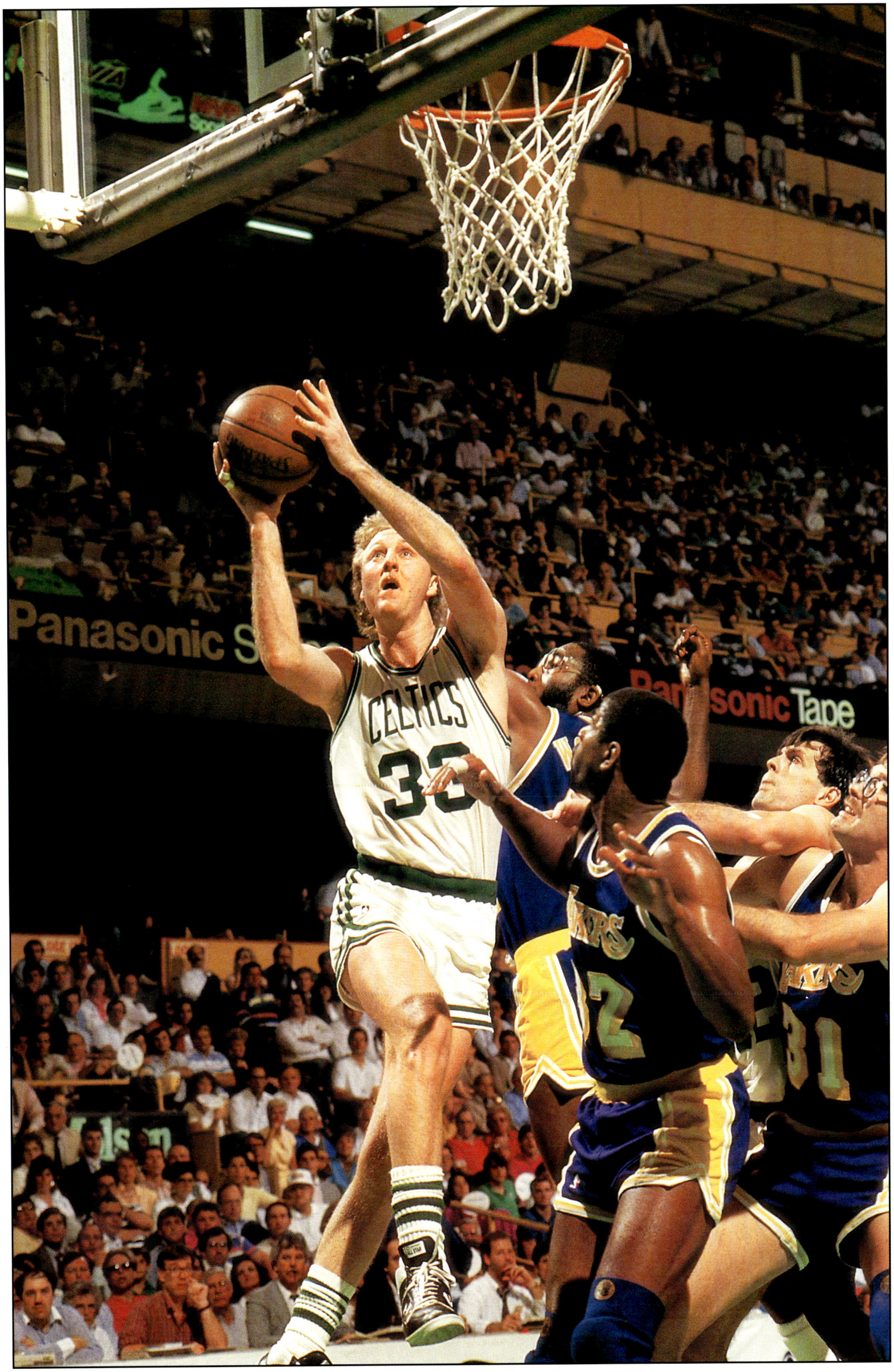

Panasonic
CELTICS
33
Tape
31

BIRD: Portrait of a Competitor

M.L. Carr off the bench, making for a deep, solid rotation. But then, as now, Boston's strength was its frontcourt. Cedric Maxwell started at power forward with Parish at center and Bird at the other corner. Off the bench came McHale, Wedman and backup center Greg Kite. There were no thin spots.

Carr and Maxwell provided their usual megadoses of spirit and banter. "Cedric was real funny," Henderson said. "Our whole team was cocky. But he was our team comedian. Him and M.L. We had a good time. It was all kiddin' around. But when the time came to get serious and win basketball games, we got serious."

"That team," Carr said of the '83-84 Celtics, "talked more junk than any team in the history of the game."

It was the perfect atmosphere for Bird. With Carr and Maxwell, Bird didn't have to be the spirited leader. Bird wasn't an outgoing person, but Maxwell and Carr drew him out and kept the proceedings loose. Later in his career, Bird would be criticized for being "distant" from his Celtic teammates. But that wasn't the case in 1983-84, Henderson said. "He was just kind of to himself. Distant could be a word for it. But he communicated on the floor, and that's where we needed him most."

The 1983-84 season would bring a rise in the level of Bird's play. The loss to Milwaukee the previous spring had provided him with a new surge of motivation. He had taken the setback personally. "It's the toughest thing that ever happened in Celtic history," he had told the writers afterward. "I'll tell you one thing, I'm going to play more basketball than ever this summer. People say, 'As Larry Bird goes, so go the Celtics.' So okay, next season I'll take on that pressure. I'll come back with more desire than ever. If it's got to start somewhere, it might as well start here."

From top to bottom, the Celtics displayed an arrogant fierceness. When an October 1983 exhibition game between the Sixers and Celtics erupted into a melee, Red Auerbach charged onto the court, took off his glasses and taunted Moses Malone. "I'm not big, hit me," Auerbach, 66 years old at the time, told Malone.

The Boston general manager was later fined $2,500 for his actions. But the mood had been set for the Celtics' season, and it was decidedly aggressive.

As a player, Jones had been a defensive mind, and that carried over to his coaching approach. He studied opposing players and had a knack for identifying weaknesses. While the rest of the league was thinking of defense in terms of steals and flashy plays, Jones was building a team mentality.

"We used to just flat-out stop people," Henderson said.

They would shut them down at one end and burn them at the other, then snicker while running back downcourt. That act gave them a league-best 62 wins over the course of the regular season. With each victory, their overbearing confidence thickened, which was fortunate because they would need it in the playoffs.

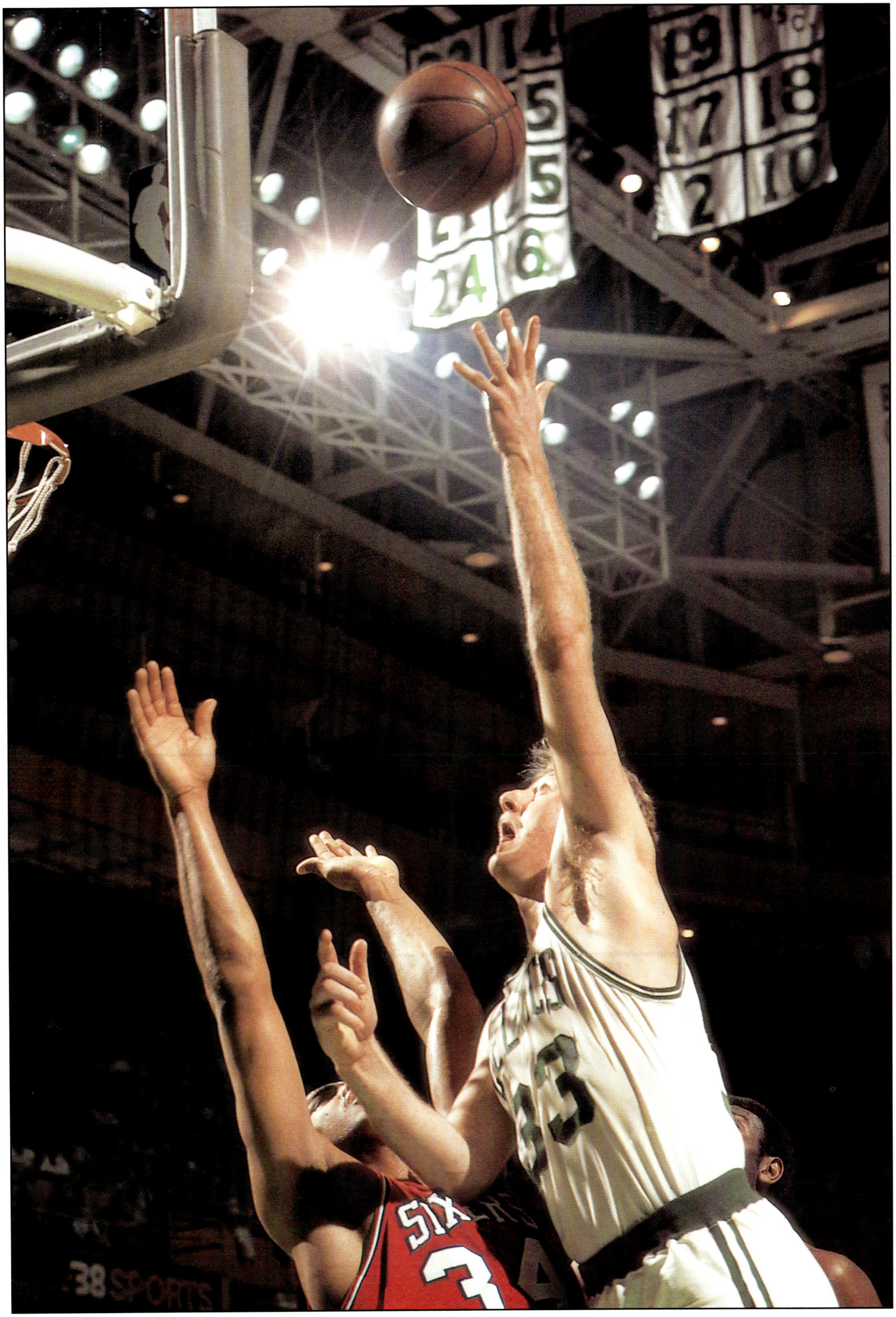

The arrival of Robert Parish in 1980 meant that he and Bird would become one of the greatest pick-and-roll combos of all time.

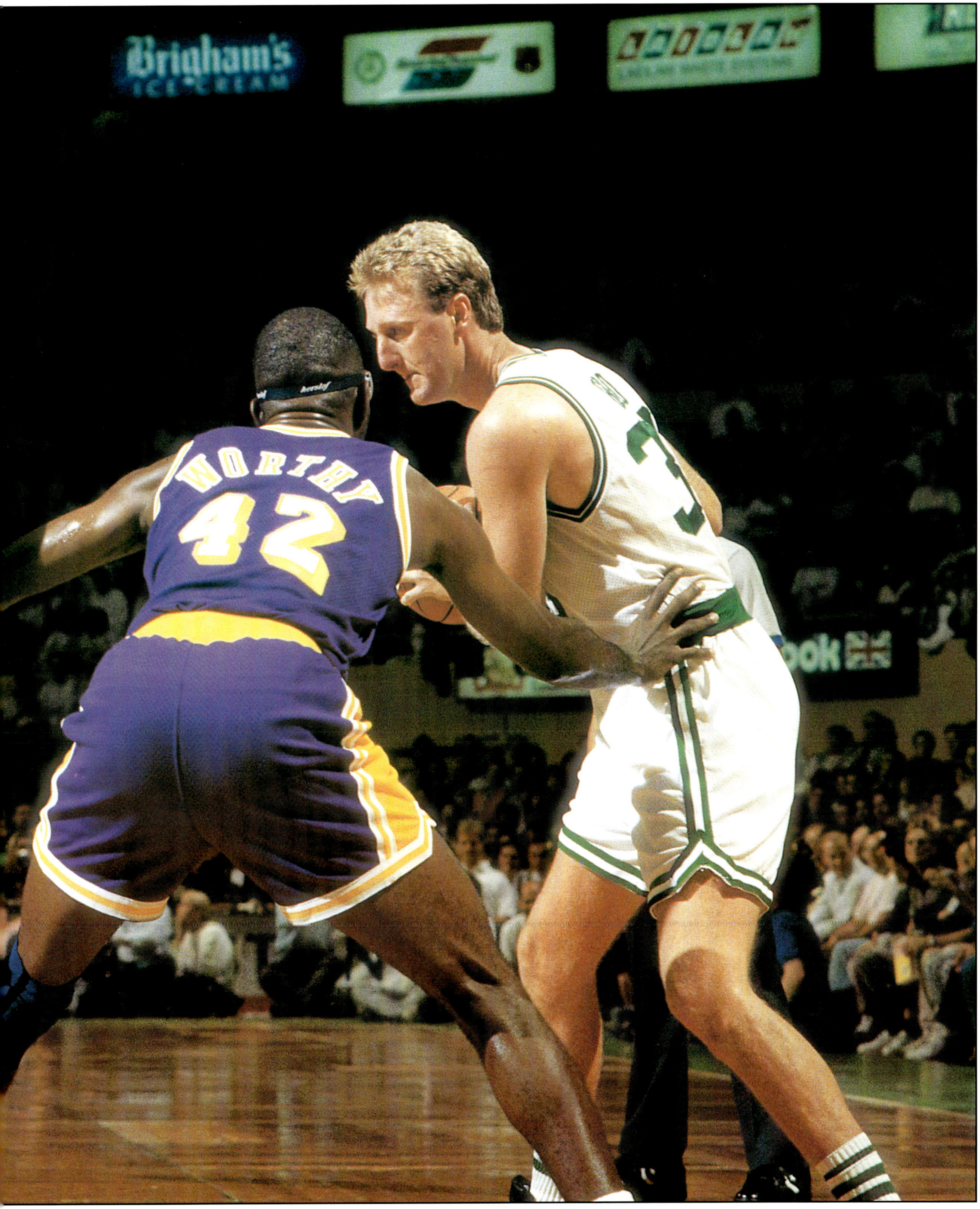
Brigham's
ICE CREAM
WORTHY
42

BIRD: Portrait of a Competitor

The Celtics brushed by Washington in the first round only to run into major problems with Bernard King and the Knicks in the Eastern semifinals. Finally they vanquished New York in seven games and enjoyed a thorough 4-1 whipping of Milwaukee in the conference finals.

Shortly thereafter, Los Angeles finished off the Phoenix Suns and took the Western Conference title. Like the Celtics, the Lakers had been through some changes. They had been swept by Philadelphia in the 1983 Finals, which left team executive Jerry West figuring ways for a quick reshuffle. Finally during the 1983-84 preseason, he sent starting guard Norm Nixon and reserve Eddie Jordan to the San Diego Clippers for backup center Swen Nater and the draft rights to rookie guard Byron Scott, out of Arizona State. In short time, the 6'4" Scott would work right into the Laker backcourt, and Showtime would be off and running again.

With injuries and other problems, the Lakers had finished the regular season at 54-28. But after Magic put an early season finger injury behind him, they won 56 of their last 61 games, including a nice little roll through the early rounds of the playoffs. As the Finals opened, there was a sense that Los Angeles was the better team. K.C. Jones said nearly as much. "The Lakers are more talented than we are," he concluded in an obvious attempt to get any psychological advantage possible.

The Boston advantage was thought to be rest and the homecourt. The Celtics had ended their conference finals series on May 23, while the Lakers didn't wrap things up until Friday night, May 25. With the first game of the Finals set for Sunday May 27 in Boston Garden, the Celtics' four days rest seemed to be a major factor. From the Laker perspective, the situation was laced with tension. It had been 15 years since Los Angeles had last faced Boston in the Finals, yet the numbers were on everyone's mind. Seven times the Lakers had met the Celtics for the championship, and seven times the Lakers had lost.

Hours before Game 1, Kareem Abdul-Jabbar was wracked by one of the migraine headaches that had troubled him throughout his career. Team trainer Jack Curran worked the center's neck and back an hour before game time, at one point popping a vertebrae into place. That seemed to do the trick on the 37-year-old captain. He walked out and treated the Garden crowd to 32 points, eight rebounds, five assists, two blocks and a steal. He made 12 of his 17 shots from the floor and eight of nine free throws. He did all of that only when the Lakers slowed down. They spent the rest of the time running their break in one door and out another for a 115-109 win.

Kaput went Boston's homecourt edge.

Game 2 then became a James Worthy showcase,. at least for the first 47 minutes or so. He hit 11 of 12 from the floor and scored 29 points. Even better, the Lakers had come from behind to take a 115-113 lead with 18 seconds left. McHale went to the free throw line for two shots, but missed both. Thoughts of sweep city crossed 14,890 Boston minds. But the Lakers picked that particular moment for a snooze. Pat Riley had told Magic to call timeout if McHale made the shots. But Magic misunderstood and called timeout after the misses, which gave Boston time to set up the defense. Inbounding at midcourt, Magic tossed the ball to Worthy, who spied Byron Scott across the court and attempted to get the ball to him. Lurking in the background praying for just such an opportunity was Henderson. He stepped in, snatched the fat pass and loped down the court for the layin. The game was tied, but again Magic made a mistake. He allowed the clock to run down without attempting a final shot.

"The other players never did anything to help him," Riley would say later in defense of Magic. "They stood out on the perimeter and didn't get open. Kareem moved with 12 seconds left, which meant he was open too early. Magic got blamed."

Late in overtime, Henderson found Wedman on the baseline and got him the ball. From there, the reserve forward put down the key jumper to give Boston a 124-121 win and a 1-1 tie in the series.

"I guess what I'll be remembered for in my career is that steal," Henderson said in 1990. "People mention it to me

Garden Glory

all the time. But even in that same game, in overtime, I like the play where I set up Scott Wedman to make the winning jumper. That goes unnoticed, but I appreciate that play more than the steal. Those were the two points that won the game."

Pat Riley's memory, however, was affixed on the steal. "What will I remember most from this series?" he asked rhetorically afterward. "Simple. Game 2. Worthy's pass to Scott. I could see the seams of the ball, like it was spinning in slow motion, but I couldn't do anything about it."

However deep their disappointment, the Lakers quickly recovered back home in the Forum. Magic had a Finals-record 21 assists, and Showtime rolled to a 137-104 win. Bird was outraged at Boston's flat performance. "We played like a bunch of sissies," he said afterward. "I know the heart and soul of this team, and today the heart wasn't there, that's for sure. I can't believe a team like this would let L.A. come out and push us around like they did. Today I didn't feel we played hard. We got beat bad, and it's very embarrassing."

The next day the Los Angeles papers began touting Worthy as the series MVP, a development that infuriated the Boston players. None was angrier than Dennis Johnson, who had scored only four points in Game 3. "I thought I was into the game," he said, "but Game 3 convinced me I wasn't. Even K.C. had to come over and ask what was wrong. I told him whatever it was, it wouldn't be there again. It was a case of getting mentally and physically aggressive."

The same was true for the entire team. Jones adjusted the team's defense, switching D.J. to cover Magic, and they went back at it. The Lakers took an early lead and seemed poised to again run off with the game. From the bench, Carr vociferously lobbied for the Celtics to become more physical. McHale complied in the second quarter when he clotheslined Kurt Rambis on a breakaway, causing a ruckus under the basket. The incident awakened the Celtics and gave the Lakers reason to pause.

Later Riley would call the Celtics "a bunch of thugs."

Maxwell, on the other hand, was overjoyed with the development. "Before Kevin McHale hit Kurt Rambis, the Lakers were just running across the street whenever they wanted," he said. "Now they stop at the corner, push the button, wait for the light and look both ways."

Still, Los Angeles held a five-point lead with less than a minute to play in regulation. But Parish stole a bad pass from Magic, and the Laker point guard later missed two key free throws, allowing the Celtics to force an overtime. Late in the extra period. Worthy faced a key free throw. But Carr hooted loudly from the bench that he would miss. Worthy did, and Maxwell stepped up and greeted him with the choke sign. The Celtics vaulted to a 129-125 win to tie the series again and regain the homecourt edge.

The free throw misses and the turnover would trouble Magic for a long time. "I thought the free throws more than the pass were mistakes," he would say later. "Those were things I—not the team—I should have taken care of. When you miss the shots you go home and sit in the dark."

The Celtics realized they were on to something. The Lakers could be intimidated. "We had to go out and make some things happen," Henderson recalled of Game 4. "If being physical was gonna do it, then we had to do it. I remember in the fourth game that was the turnaround. We had to have that game or we were gonna be down 3-1. We had to have it. We had guys who could make some things happen."

Dennis Johnson was certainly one of those guys. After struggling early in the series, he would finish the final four games by scoring 22, 22, 20 and 22 points. Bird, too, fit that make-things-happen mold, particularly in Game 5 back in Boston.

Boston Globe writer Bob Ryan had seen Bird perform in many situations but listed the fifth game of that '84 series as his favorite. "The so-called 'heat game' in 1984," he said. "The fifth game with Los Angeles. It was 97 degrees in the Boston Garden, and the one player that you could have predicted turned this game into a positive was Larry Bird. That sums up Larry Bird. The Lakers were sitting there sucking on oxygen and Bird is saying, 'Hey, we've all

BIRD: Portrait of a Competitor

played outdoors in the summer. We've all played on asphalt. We've all done this. Why should this be different? It's just because we have uniforms on and it's a national television audience.' That game and that performance summed up Bird to me as much as anything else he's ever done."

In that crucial match, Bird was 15 for 20 from the floor for 34 points as Boston won, 121-103. Kareem, meanwhile, had appeared to be just what he was—a 37-year-old man running in sweltering heat. How hot was it? a reporter asked.

Garden Glory

BIRD: Portrait of a Competitor

Boston outdueled Los Angeles for the 1984 title.

"I suggest," Kareem replied, "that you go to a local steam bath, do 100 pushups with all your clothes on, and then try to run back and forth for 48 minutes. The game was in slow motion. It was like we were running in mud."

"I love to play in the heat," Bird said, smiling. "I just run faster, create my own wind."

"He was just awesome," Riley said of Bird. "He made everything work."

But it wasn't just Bird. The Celtics were a full-blown team. "This is probably the best game we ever played," D.J. said.

The Lakers then answered the Celtics' aggressiveness in Game 6 back in the air-conditioned Forum. In the first period, Worthy shoved Maxwell into a basket support. From there, the Lakers rode their newfound toughness and an old standby. Kareem scored 30, and Los Angeles pulled away down the stretch for a 119-108 win to tie the series at three apiece. As Carr left the Forum floor, a fan pitched a cup of liquid in his face, enraging the Celtics. Carr said afterward that the Lakers had declared "all-out war." Bird suggested that the Lakers better wear their hard hats for Game 7 in the Garden.

The entire city of Boston was juiced up for the event that Tuesday night, June 12. The Lakers needed a police escort to get from their hotel to North Station, the subway station that adjoined the Garden. Carr came out wearing goggles to mock Kareem, and told the Lakers they weren't going to win. Not in the Garden.

Maxwell further ensured that, telling his teammates to put the load on his back because he was ready to carry them. Which he did. He presented a high-action low-post puzzle that the Lakers never solved. He demoralized them on the offensive boards. He drew fouls. By halftime, he had made 11 of 13 free throws. When they tried to double-team him, he passed them silly. He finished with 24 points, eight assists and eight rebounds. Bird had 20 points and 12 rebounds, Parish 14 points and 16 rebounds. And D.J. was majestic again with 22 points.

Even against that barrage, the Lakers fought back from a 14-point deficit to trail by just three with more than a minute left. Magic had the ball, but D.J. knocked it loose. Michael Cooper recovered it for L.A. Magic again went to work and spied Worthy open under the basket. But before Magic could make the pass, Maxwell knocked the ball away yet again. Later the vision of Worthy open under the basket would return to Magic again and again.

At the other end, D.J. drew a foul and made the shots, spurring the Celtics to their 15th championship, 111-102. Bird was named the MVP after averaging 27.4 points, 14 rebounds, 3.2 assists and two steals over the series. But Maxwell's seventh-game performance had been incredible. And once again Dennis Johnson had delivered in the clutch.

All of which was celebrated deliriously by the Garden crowd.

"We worked hard for this," Bird said in the din of the locker room afterward. "Anybody gonna say we didn't earn it?"

BIRD: Portrait of a Competitor

At age 28, Bird flexed his talent during the 1984-85 regular season, averaging 28.7 points, 10.5 rebounds and 6.6 assists per game. The Celtics, though, were not as strong. Henderson had held out for more money over the summer, so Boston traded him to Seattle. General Manager Jan Volk explained that the team figured Danny Ainge had progressed enough to carry the starting load. Yet there was no doubt the trade left the Celtics thin. Maxwell, too, had held out for more money, and the Celtics eventually came up with a new contract. But during the season, the power forward was troubled by chronic knee problems that eventually required exploratory surgery. In his absence, McHale moved from sixth man to starter. Observers noted that the Celtic starters—Bird, Kevin McHale, Dennis Johnson, Danny Ainge and Robert Parish—had averaged better than 2,500 minutes of playing time over the season.

The Lakers, on the other hand, had come back with a fierceness and were once again a deep, talented team. By playoff time, the frontcourt was bolstered by the return of Mitch Kupchak and Jamaal Wilkes to go with Kareem, Worthy, Rambis, McAdoo and Larry Spriggs. The backcourt showed Magic, Scott, Cooper and McGee. As a group, the Lakers were driven by their '84 humiliation.

"Those wounds from last June stayed open all summer," Riley said as the playoffs neared. "Now the misery has subsided, but it never leaves your mind completely."

With a 63-19 regular-season finish, the Celtics had again claimed the home-court advantage. The Lakers had finished 62-20. And neither team dallied in the playoffs. Boston dismissed Cleveland, Detroit and Philadelphia in quick succession. The Lakers rolled past Phoenix, Portland and Denver.

For the first time in years, the Finals returned to a 2-3-2 format, with the first two games in Boston, the middle three in Los Angeles, and the last two, if necessary, back in Boston. The situation set up an immense opportunity for the Lakers to steal one in the Garden, then pressure the Celtics back in Los Angeles. However it would be done, Magic, Kareem and company figured on rectifying their humiliation from 1984.

Little did they know they would have to suffer one final, profound embarrassment. Game 1 opened on Memorial Day, Monday May 27, with both teams cruising on five days rest since closing out their conference duties the previous Wednesday night. The Lakers, however, quickly took on the appearance of guys who had just come off two weeks on the graveyard shift. The 38-year-old Kareem, in particular, slogged up and down the court, while Robert Parish seemed to glide. Often Kareem would just be reaching the top of the key to catch up, when all of a sudden the action raced the other way. He finished the day with 12 points and three rebounds. And Magic had only one rebound. Meanwhile, the famed Showtime running game had been slowed to a belly crawl.

And the Celtics?

They placed a huge red welt on the Lakers' scar from the previous year, 148-114. Scott Wedman hit 11 for 11 from the floor, including four thee-pointers. But it was Danny Ainge who had lashed the whip, lacing in six straight buckets at the end of the first quarter to finish the period with 15 points. "It was one of those days," K.C. Jones said, "where if you turn around and close your eyes, the ball's gonna go in."

For all their success, the Celtics suddenly quieted their trash talking, as if they sensed that they had gone too far. They hadn't expected it to be this easy. And the last thing they wanted to do was rile the Lakers. "It's definitely time to back off," Maxwell said. "It's not like backgammon or cribbage, where if you beat someone bad enough you get two wins."

But it was too late. The teams didn't play again until Thursday, and there was an uneasy air in Boston despite the big win.

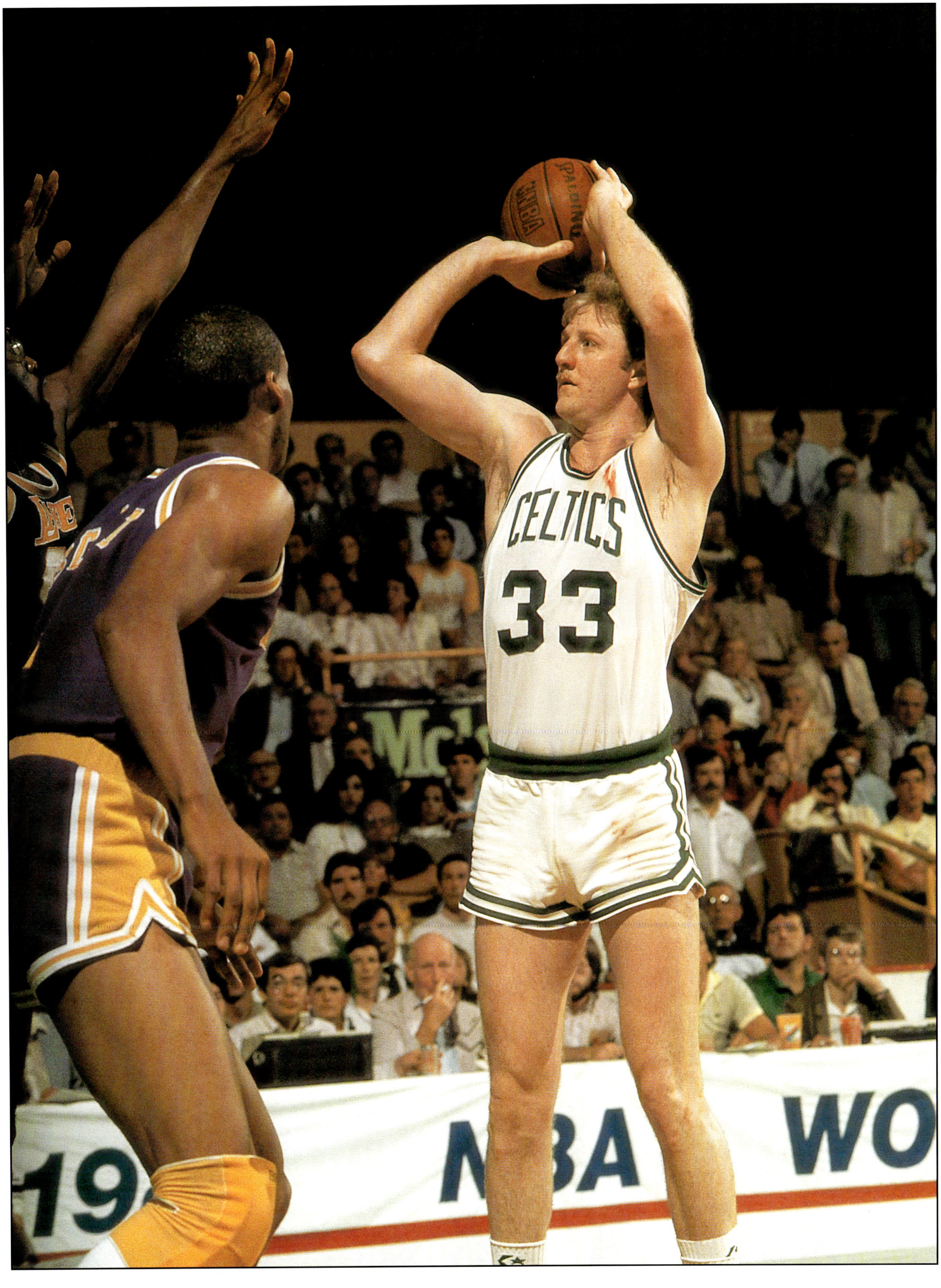
CELTICS
33

BIRD: Portrait of a Competitor

Kareem, in particular, reasserted himself in Game 2 with 30 points, 17 rebounds, eight assists and three blocks. Cooper hit eight of nine from the floor to finish with 22 points. And like that, the Lakers evened the series, 109-102. Best of all, they had stolen a game in the Garden, and now returned to the Forum for three straight.

L. A. expected us to crawl into a hole," Lakers assistant Dave Wohl said of the Celtics. "It's like the bully on the block who keeps taking your lunch money every day. Finally you get tired of it and you whack him."

They hosted the Celtics on Sunday afternoon and really whacked 'em again, returning the favor of Game 1, 136-111. This time Worthy was the man, with 29 points. But Kareem's presence was felt again, too. He had 26 points and 14 rebounds.

At one point, Boston had led, 48-38, but Worthy dominated the second quarter and charged Los Angeles to a 65-59 edge at intermission. The Lakers ran away in the second half, during which Kareem became the league's all-time leading playoff scorer with 4,458 points.

Bird, meanwhile, had fallen into a two-game shooting slump, going 17 for 42. He had been troubled by a chronically sore right elbow and bad back, although some speculated his real trouble was Cooper's defense. Bird confirmed as much by refusing to offer excuses.

As with '84, the series was marked by physical play, although this time around it seemed to be the Lakers who were determined to gain an intimidation edge. "We're not out to physically harm them," Kareem offered. "But I wouldn't mind hurting their feelings." Before Game 4, the NBA's vice president of operations, Scotty Stirling, warned each coach that fighting and extra rough play would be met with fines and suspensions. Riley told his players of Stirling's warning, but K.C. Jones chose not to. With their uninhibited play, the Celtics gained an edge, and the close game

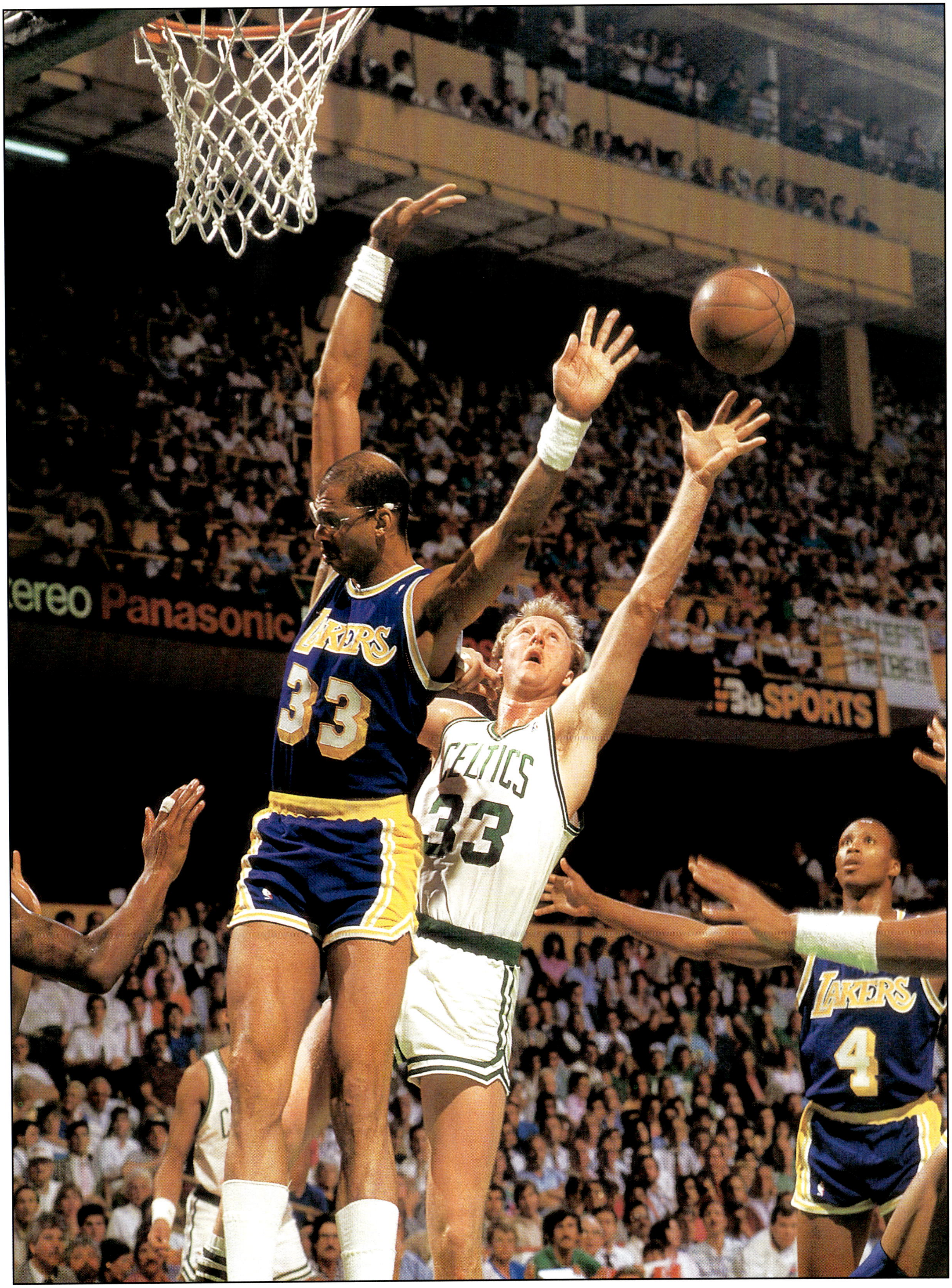
tereo
Panasonic
LAKERS
33
CELTICS
33
SPORTS
LAKERS
4

Home Video Recorder

Garden Glory

came down to one final Celtic possession. Bird had the ball but faced a double-team, so he dumped it off to D. J. above the foul line. From there, Johnson drilled the winner with two seconds left. Boston had evened the series and regained its homecourt advantage, 107-105.

Game 5 two nights later in the Forum was the critical showdown. McHale answered the call for Boston, putting down 16 early points and forcing Riley to make a defensive switch in the second period. The L.A. coach put Kareem on McHale and left the shorter Rambis to contend with Parish. It worked immediately. The Lakers went on a 14-3 run at the close of the half to take a 64-51 lead. They stretched it to 89-72 after intermission, until the Celtics closed to within four at 101-97 with six minutes left. But Magic hit three shots and Kareem added four more, giving him 36 on the day, as the Lakers walked away with a 3-2 lead, 120-111.

"People didn't think we could win close games," Magic said afterward.

From there it went back to Boston, where Kareem answered again, this time with 29 points, 18 of them in the second half when it mattered. The score was tied at 55 at intermission. The Celtics had played only seven people in the first half, and Magic could see that they were tired. It was written on their faces. Riley told him to keep pushing it at them, not to worry about turnovers. Just keep up the pressure. Keep pushing.

He did.

And the Celtics did something they had never ever done before. They gave up a championship on their home floor, on the hallowed parquet, 111-100. McHale had kept them alive with 36 points, but he got his sixth foul with more than five minutes left. And, thanks in part to Cooper's defense, Bird was closing out a 12-for-29 afternoon. "I thought I'd have a great game today," he said afterward.

In the end, the Lakers' victory was signalled by the squeaking of sneakers in the deathly quiet Garden as the crowd slipped away. It was the same crowd that had so riotously jostled the Lakers the year before.

"We made 'em lose it," Magic said with satisfaction.

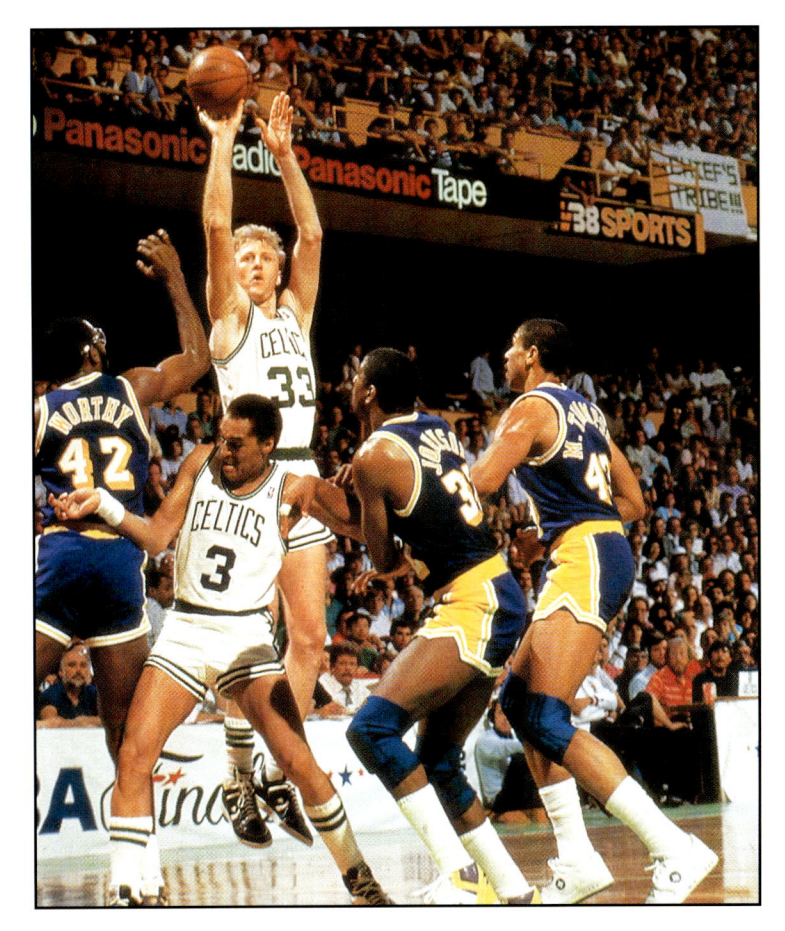

55

BIRD: Portrait of a Competitor

Far beyond even what Red Auerbach had imagined, Kevin McHale and Robert Parish gave Boston perhaps the most imposing frontcourt in the league. Teamed with Cedric Maxwell, Bird and Scott Wedman in 1984, the Celtics could present problems in every facet of the game. As a group, they were brilliant and consistent scorers and superior defenders. But Maxwell's knee problems changed this special working combination in 1985. Parish and McHale put in extra minutes, and it became obvious that the team needed more depth.

It was particularly obvious to Bill Walton. The former Portland center had traveled basketball's hard road since leading the Trail Blazers to the 1977 NBA title. Foot injuries and foot reconstruction operations had virtually taken him out of the game, leaving his career a frustrating chain of stops and starts. He had left the Trail Blazers in 1978 and eventually dropped out of basketball, opting instead to attend law school at Stanford. He later discovered that he had healed enough to play part-time for the San Diego Clippers. His feet didn't feel too bad in 1985, and he got the notion that perhaps he could help the Celtics, the team that he had always admired. As a backup to Parish, Walton figured he could play just enough to give the team quality center play while Parish or McHale rested. Walton contacted Red Auerbach, who consulted Larry Bird, who thought it was a great idea. Shortly thereafter, the Celtics traded Maxwell to the Clippers for Big Bill.

It was the kind of deal that brought immediate scrutiny. Why would the Celtics want to gamble on Walton when every season brought a recurrence of the injuries? The answer became apparent just a matter of games into the 1985-86 schedule—Boston had combined the greatest passing center with the greatest passing forward in the game. The result was an exhibition of ball movement and team play that left the rest of the NBA in another class. In December, the Celtics lost a game to Portland in Boston Garden. It would be their only home loss of the year.

At the heart of their performamce was a team hunger, almost a craziness.

Guard Jerry Sichting joined the team in the offseason and remembers being amazed at the intensity level when Boston traveled to Los Angeles for a preseason game in October 1985. It was as if the Finals competition had resumed immediately, only stronger. While Kareem Abdul-Jabbar and Walton had both played at UCLA, they held no lost love for each other.

The electric atmosphere in the Forum that night soon transformed into lightning, and a fight quickly broke out that resulted in a massive on-court pileup.

Sichting remembers the officials untangling the pile to find Boston coach K.C. Jones, rumpled suit and all, at the very bottom.

It was then, Sichting said, that he realized he was about to catch a ride on a whirlwind.

The Celtics roared out on a winning tear that converted doubters at every stop. "Right now, there's no doubt that Boston is a much better team," Magic Johnson said in February 1986 after the Celtics beat the Lakers in the Forum to extend their record to 41-9. On their way to a club-record 67-15 season, the Celtics would claim a winning record against every team in the league.

Few people foresaw this amazing turnaround, including Bird, who had contemplated sitting out the '86 season because of back pain. But the acquisition of Walton and Sichting from Indiana had convinced him it would be wise to hang around and see how things turned out. His reward was the kind of season that only superstars can dream about. He averaged 25.8 points and nearly seven assists, two steals and 10 rebounds per game. He shot .423 from three-point range and finished first in the league in free-throw percentage. For the second consecutive season, Bird broke the

Garden Glory

2,000-point mark. And he finished the year with 10 triple-doubles.

At the All-Star game in Dallas in February, Bird had 23 points, seven steals, eight rebounds and five assists.

Despite a sore Achilles tendon that forced him to miss 14 games in the middle of the season, McHale responded to his first year as a full-time starter by averaging 21.3 points. His .574 field-goal percentage was fifth best in the league. He blocked 134 shots during the regular season and another 43 during the playoffs. The former two-time Sixth Man award winner was named to the All-Star team and to the NBA All-Defensive first team.

Walton, meanwhile, jumped into McHale's vacancy and claimed the Sixth Man award. He played 80 regular season games for the Celtics (a career high for Walton) and gave them 20 minutes per outing. He shot .562 from the floor and had 162 assists.

The team's other acquisition, Sichting, shot an amazing .570 from the floor as a backcourt sub.

And Parish averaged 9.5 rebounds and 16.1 points per game while shooting .549 from the floor. On occasion, he and Walton played side-by-side in a twin towers setup. The towers became triplets at times when McHale joined them in the lineup. And if K.C. Jones didn't need size, he could go to a smaller, quicker group with Bird, Wedman and McHale. The backcourt had similar depth with Ainge, Dennis Johnson, Sichting, David Thirdkill and Rick Carlisle, all of whom contributed minutes, scoring and defense.

The season took an unexpected turn when Houston eliminated the Lakers in the Western Conference Finals, 4-1. Los Angeles had reshuffled its lineup, releasing Robert McAdoo and Jamaal Wilkes, and picking up veteran power forward Maurice Lucas in a trade and rookie A.C. Green through the draft. The Lakers got off to a good start on their way to a 62-20 record, but the chemistry wasn't there in the spring.

The Rockets, on the other hand, played with confidence and enthusiasm. With Bill Fitch as coach, they sported their own twin towers, 7'4" Ralph Sampson at forward and 6'11" Hakeem Olajuwon at center. Jim Petersen was the backup power forward, while Robert Reid and Rodney McCray worked the other corner. The guards included Mitch Wiggins, Allen Leavell and Lewis Lloyd. John Lucas had played most of the season in the backcourt, but fell by the wayside with a springtime recurrence of his drug problem. The Rockets, though, adjusted to this setback and claimed the Midwest Division title with a 51-31 record. They ousted Sacramento and Denver rather quickly before losing the first game against the Lakers in the Forum, then coming back to sweep four straight. Their

Houston fans razz Bird over Robert Reid's defense during '86 finals.

fourth victory against Los Angeles came on a buzzer-beating, turnaround jumper by Sampson in the Forum. Houston had set up the final play with a mere second on the clock. Sampson caught the inbounds pass, whirled and released. The ball hit the rim, bounded high, and fell right to the bottom of Laker hearts.

Boston scorched Chicago 3-0, Atlanta, 4-1, and Milwaukee, 4-0, in a searing playoff drive, then had to wait eight days for the Finals to begin on Monday, May 26. The Celtics were highly favored, and for good reason. For the Rockets to win, Sampson had to play well, which didn't always happen. A solid defensive rebounder with a soft shooting touch and excellent mobility and quickness for a big man, Sampson had been plagued by inconsistency since becoming the top pick in the 1983 draft. He had also been prone to foul trouble at times.

In Game 1, both of those plagues returned. And they weren't pretty. Sampson picked up his third foul just five minutes into the first period. He spent the rest of the half on the bench, and when he did return in the second half, he missed 12 of his first 13 shots. Olajuwon tried to compensate for Sampson's absence with 33 points and 12 rebounds. But McHale and Parish powered around the frontcourt at will, while Bird polished his all-around game with 21 points, 13 assists, eight rebounds and four steals. His double-teaming on Olajuwon helped frustrate the Rockets further.

The Celtics shot 66 percent from the floor for the game. Ainge and Johnson had a big third quarter, and the whole

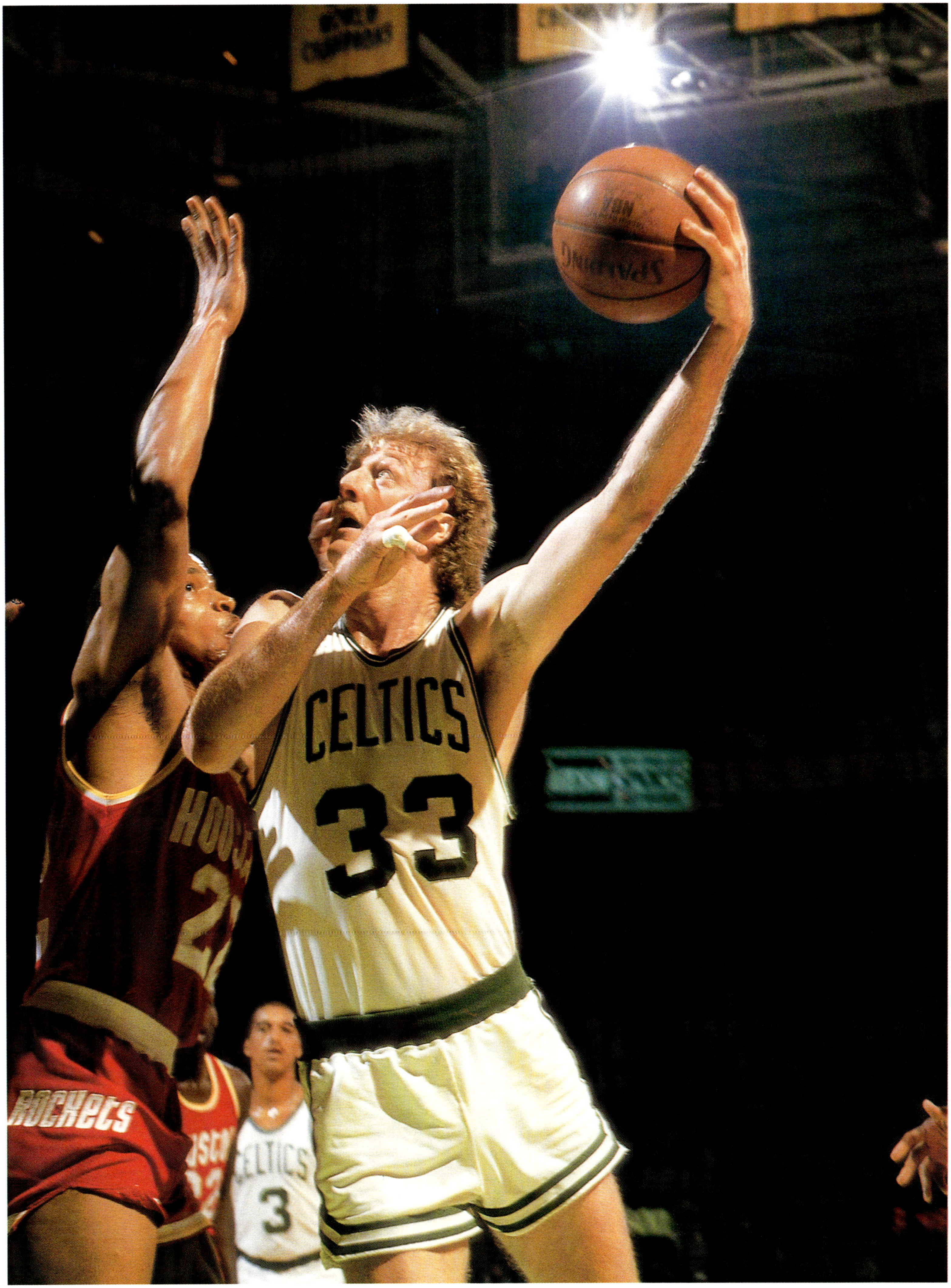
CELTICS
33
ROCKETS
CELTICS
3

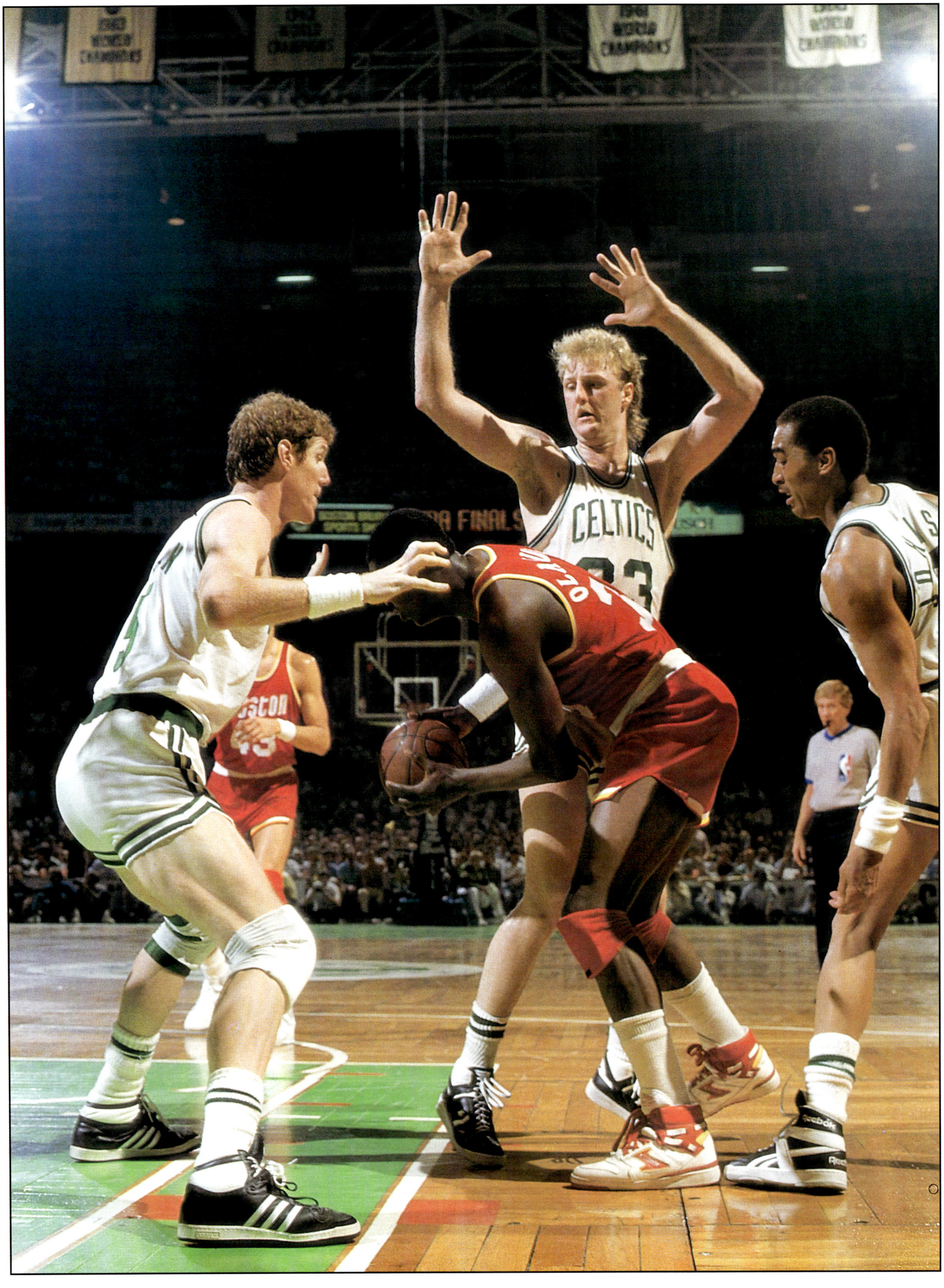
CELTICS
Reebok

Garden Glory

team floated on a high-octane confidence. They won, 112-100, and privately wondered if they weren't headed for another sweep.

That untouchable mentality carried right through Game 2, in which Bird failed to pick up a single foul despite double-teaming Olajuwon much of the game. He did, however, get 31 points, eight rebounds, seven assists, four steals and two blocks. He worked McCray over on offense, backing in to take any of an assortment of shots or working the pick-and-roll with Parish. Sampson played better and finished with 18 points and eight rebounds. But he still seemed intimidated by Boston Garden. The Celtics ran away with the third quarter, 34-19, and won it, 117-95.

Bird's performance had left Olajuwon awestruck. "He's the greatest player I've ever seen," the Houston center told reporters. Still, Olajuwon said that once the Rockets got back to Houston for the next three games, he didn't see how the Celtics could beat them in the Summit.

In the time off between venues, Bird received his MVP award. And once in the Summit, he again rang up big numbers—25 points, 15 rebounds, 11 assists and four steals. Running their break smoothly, the Celtics seemed in control in the third period with a 76-65 lead. But then Fitch switched Robert Reid to cover Bird, and the Boston forward shot three for 12 in the second half. On offense, Sampson found his comfort zone and powered Houston into the lead in the fourth period. He finished with 24 points and 22 rebounds. In the closing minutes, the Rockets ripped through a 9-0 run and took a 103-102 lead with 67 seconds to go. Boston regained the lead when Ainge scored. But Wiggins answered on a tap-in, and then the Houston defense forced Boston into a bad shot. Later Parish stepped on the sideline as Boston was inbouding the ball, and Houston survived, 106-104.

"They got lucky," Bird said.

Game 4, of course, was the test. Parish faced down Houston's big men to lead Boston with 22 points and 10 rebounds. Then Bird took over in prime time. With the score tied at 101 and a little over two minutes left, he threw in a trey. Then on a last-minute Boston possession, Walton rammed home an offensive rebound. Combined, the scores gave the Celtics a 106-103 win and a 3-1 lead in the series.

Game 5, on Thursday, June 5, is remembered for a silly fight between Sampson and Sichting. With a little more than three minutes gone in the second period, the Houston forward and Boston's reserve guard got tangled up over the ball. They had words, which led to Sampson throwing punches, one of which struck D.J. in the left eye when he attempted to break things up. Sichting later joked that his sister hit harder than Sampson and that he wasn't sure whether the blow was "a punch or a mosquito bite." But the outburst resulted in Sampson's ejection. Rather than fold, the Rockets found motivation in the incident. They got inspired backup play from Petersen. And Olajuwon put on a grand show with 32 points, 14 rebounds and eight blocks. In the end, the Celtics weren't sure what they had stirred up in Houston, but they knew they didn't want to stir it again. The Rockets blasted 'em, 111-96, and the series stood at 3-2. Fortunately for the Celtics, it was headed back to Boston Garden, where their combined record for the regular and post season was 49-1.

As expected, the Beantown crowd was ready to ambush Sampson for Game 6. When the Rockets got off their team bus for the shootaround that morning, they were greeted by the jeers of a rowdy gathering. And before game time, Celtics radio announcer Johnny Most roasted Sampson as gutless and yellow, and every time the Houston forward touched the ball, the Garden regulars booed to their hearts' delight. "Sampson Is A Sissy" read one poster. "Sampson you fight like Delilah," read another. The atmosphere made for a tough time for Ralph. He missed his first seven shots before punctuating his frustration with a dunk in the second period. On the day, he would total only eight points.

"I just played bad," a dejected Sampson said later when asked if the crowd had affected him.

Bird, meanwhile, was afire, yelling at his teammates, pushing the action and diving for loose balls. He finished the first half with 16 points, eight rebounds and eight assists to give Boston a 55-38 lead. His teammates knew he wanted the ball. "Just by getting mad and storming around, I got everybody's attention," he said later. "I didn't want this day to slip away from me."

It didn't.

In the third period he sharpened the heart stakes, driving home a flurry of three-point shots. That and Boston's swarming defense sent the Rockets down hard. The Celtics led by 30 in the fourth period and went on to claim their 16th championship, 114-97. On the day, Bird rang up 29 points, 11 rebounds, 12 assists and three steals. The player that Bill Fitch had initiated into the league had disassembled his old coach's new team. Nobody appreciated his performance more than Fitch himself.

"Once the lights go out and play starts, the crowd has more effect on Larry than anyone I've ever seen," the Houston coach said. "I've never seen him more intense than he was today."

(At his retirement, Bird conceded that his emotions had never been higher than before Game 6 in 1986. "I never had a feeling like that before in my life," he said. "My heart was pounding so hard, I thought I was having a heart

> **"I never had a feeling like that before in my life," he said. "My heart was pounding so hard, I thought I was having a heart attack. I loved it [playing at that level], but I never got there again."**

attack. I loved it [playing at that level], but I never got there again.")

"He is undoubtedly, in my mind at least, the best basketball player playing the game today," Dennis Johnson told reporters afterward. Despite the praise, Bird played the perfectionist. "I've got some things to work on," he said. "I'm not real comfortable with my moves to the basket. By next fall, I want four or five moves I can go to. If I do that, I think I'll be unstoppable."

As a team, Boston had concluded its most impressive season. The Garden parquet had never been more hallowed. Throughout the regular season and the playoffs, the Celtics had run up a 50-1 homecourt record. The image, of course, was that they had done it with their Bird-led offense. But their defense, in particular, had befuddled the Rockets. "I don't remember the last time I was hounded by a team more than I was today," Sampson said. "Every time I touched the ball, there were two and three guys around me. And that went for Akeem, too."

None of the defense was accidental, K.C. Jones said with pride. "Our defensive intensity was phenomenal. We contested every pass and every dribble. They were under constant pressure every time they touched the ball."

With their third championship, Bird and his Celtics had evened the ring count with Magic and his Lakers. The balance of the decade was there for the taking, and both sides knew it. The Celtics, though, figured they were developing an edge. Due to the 1984 Gerald Henderson trade with Seattle, Boston had the number two overall pick in the 1986 draft. With it, Red Auerbach planned to select Maryland forward Len Bias. He wasn't another Michael Jordan, but many observers thought he was close. And he would be just the infusion of talent and athleticisim to put the Celtics back on top.

Larry and his teammates shoved aside Houston to claim Boston's 16th championship in 1986.

Boston celebrates the '86 title.

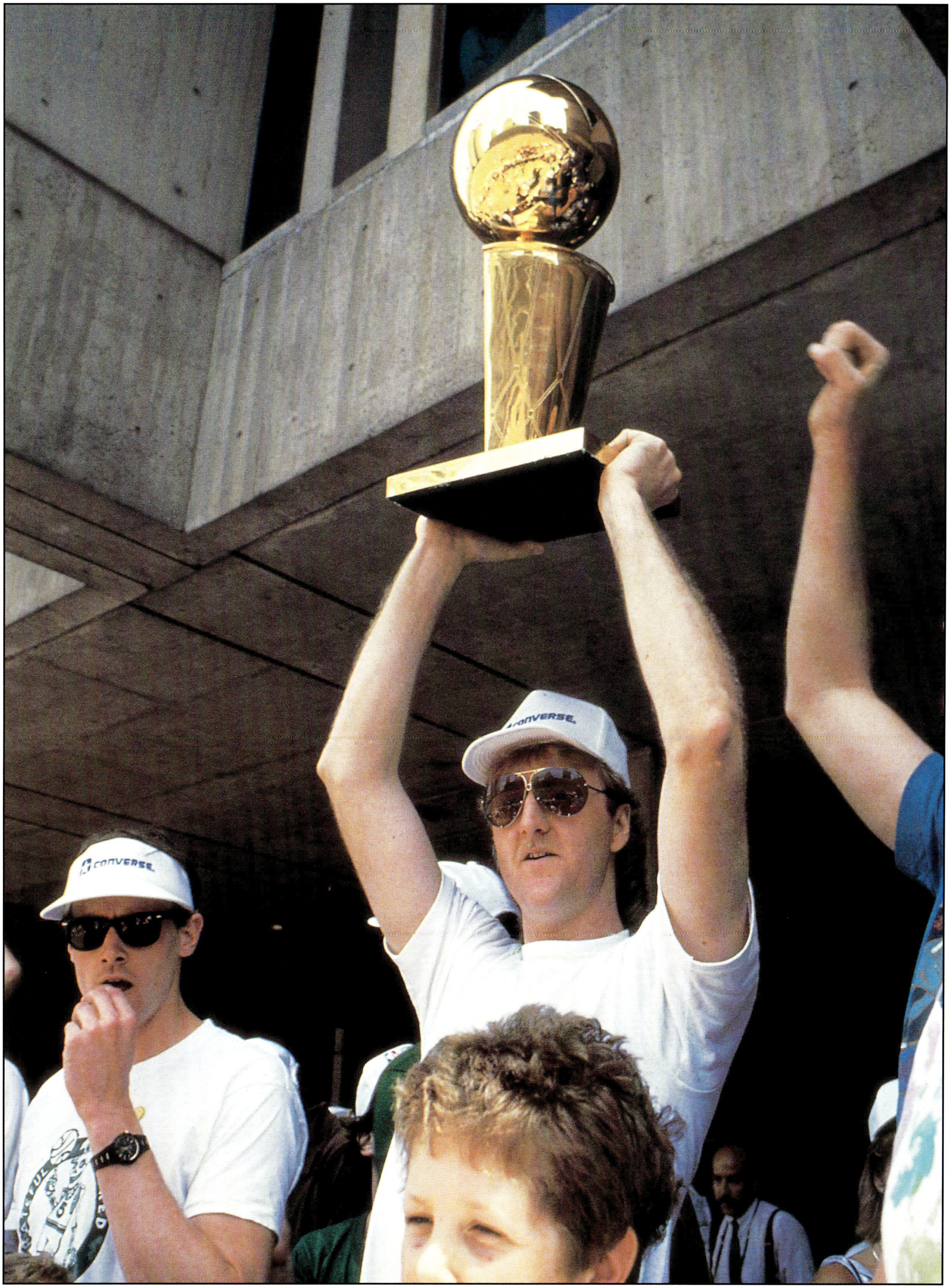
CONVERSE
CONVERSE

BIRD: Portrait of a Competitor

The Rubber Match

It had been 18 seasons since any team had won back-to-back championships in the NBA. The 1986-87 Celtics had hopes of being the first modern team to stretch to that achievement. But, one-by-one, things fell apart for them. Tragedy struck the day after the draft when Len Bias, the second player chosen behind Brad Daugherty, collapsed and died from cocaine-induced heart failure. From what investigators could determine, the incident was either the first time, or among the first times, Bias had used the drug. Yet it cost him his life and destroyed the Celtics' future plans. Like that, the second pick of the first round was gone. From there, the team's troubles came in waves.

The Boston bench, which seemed so deep in 1986, rapidly disintegrated. After an early-season accident on a stationary bike, Bill Walton was sidelined with the foot injuries that had plagued him throughout his career. Scott Wedman was struck down by a heel injury and never played for Boston again, and Sichting was slowed by a persistent virus. To bolster the frontcourt, the Celtics picked up Darren Daye and Fred Roberts, but they needed time to build confidence and develop. Without a strong bench, the Boston starters were forced to play Herculean minutes. As a result, Ainge, Bird and Parish were all troubled by nagging injuries. Then, late in the season, Kevin McHale broke a navicular bone in his right foot and tore ligaments as well. The doctors were worried that continued play might cause McHale permanent damage, but because the Celtics seemed to have a good chance in the playoffs, he decided to play hurt.

In time, of course, they would learn that McHale's effort didn't matter. If bad luck hadn't finished off the Celtics, Magic Johnson would find a way to get the job done. Boston finished the regular schedule at 59-23, the best in the Eastern Conference, but the Celtics quickly found themselves in one brutal playoff struggle after another.

Walton had returned in March, but his effort was almost painful to watch. He helped in the first round as Boston eliminated Chicago, 3-0. But after that, he never regained his touch and never performed well enough to contribute. Boston survived Milwaukee in a seven-game Eastern semifinal, then bashed heads with Detroit in the Eastern finals. Again the series went to seven games, and Boston escaped, but only by the virtue of Bird's last-second steal of an Isiah Thomas pass in game 5. Bird quickly fed Dennis Johnson for the winning layup, a play for the ages if there ever was one.

That, however, would just about conclude the Celtics' highlight clips for 1987.

The Lakers had home court advantage and the clear upper hand when the NBA Finals opened on Tuesday June 2, in the Forum before a crowd peppered with celebrity.

Laker coach Pat Riley figured either the Celtics would come in game-sharp and take it to the Lakers, or they would come in weary from two straight seven-game battles. The latter very quickly established itself as the operating format for the day. Their tongues wagging, the Celtics could do little more than watch the Lakers run weave drills up and down the floor. "The Celtics looked to me like they were keeping up pretty good," Laker Mychal Thompson quipped later, "just at a different pace."

The Lakers ran 35 fast breaks in the first two quarters and led by 21 at intermission. They settled into a canter thereafter, finally ending it, 126-113.

In Game 2, Boston trailed by seven in the second quarter, when Michael Cooper pushed the Lakers through a 20-10 outburst, accounting all 20 points himself by either scoring or assisting. When it was over, he had made six of seven trey attempts (a record), and his eight assists tied a Finals' record. And the Celtics had spent another day gasping in pursuit of the Laker break. "One of the Laker girls could've scored a layup on us," said backup center Greg Kite. Actually, the Lakers did quite well without the help of any of their girls. Kareem flicked in 10 of 14 shots for 23 points, while Magic put up nice boxy numbers, 20 assists and 22 points.

It all added up to a 141-122 rout, Boston's sixth straight road loss in the playoffs. The L.A. papers enjoyed these developments thoroughly and took to calling the Celtics "Gang Green."

Bird waged a furious war with the Detroit Pistons in '87.

"This was the most important game of the series for us. If we lost, it might've been tough to get up for Game 4. Now it's going to be easy."

Riley expected the worst in Game 4 and got it. Boston went up by 16 just after the half. Longtime Laker fan Jack Nicholson, who had wormed a seat in the upper press area, spent most of the evening getting choke signs from Boston fans. "There was one guy," Nicholson said. "He was giving me the choke sign so hard, I almost sent for the paramedics. He was wearing a gray sweat shirt, and his face turned almost as gray as his shirt. I couldn't believe it."

Shortly thereafter, relief came to Nicholson and the Lakers. L.A. cut the lead to eight with three and a half minutes to go in the game. From there,

Before doubt crept too far into Celtic minds, they righted themselves in Game 3. Despite his bad ankle, McHale scored 21 points with 10 rebounds to lead Boston to a 109-103 win.

For a brief moment the pressure was off the Celtics. No longer did they have to worry about the big embarrassment. "We're just too good a team to be swept," Bird said.

the conclusion, the series actually, came down to one Magic sequence.

With half a minute left, the Lakers took a 104-103 lead and a pick-and-roll to Abdul-Jabbar. But Bird grabbed it back at the 0:12 mark with a three-pointer, putting Boston up, 106-104.

On the next possession, Kareem was fouled and went to the

The Pistons presented a physical challenge in the late 1980s.

Garden Glory

line, where he made the first and missed the second. McHale grabbed the rebound, but Mychal Thompson gave him a gentle push and the ball went out of bounds. McHale signalled Boston ball, but the officials pointed the other way.

What followed, of course, was another of those plays for the ages. For years afterward, Magic Johnson would sit in the private screening room at his mansion, playing and replaying the scene thousands of times, each time tingling with a glee that would refuel his competitive fires. The play replenished his spirit every time he watched it.

Perhaps the definition of a Celtic hell is being assigned to Magic's screening room for eternity, watching the sequence and listening to his delighted laughter over and over and over.

Magic took the ball on the inbounds pass at the left of the key and at first contemplated a 20-footer, but McHale came out to change his mind. So Magic motored into the key, where Bird and Parish joined McHale in a trio of extended arms as Magic lofted a short hook. Parish almost brushed it. But the ball rose up and then descended to a swish. K.C. Jones, watching in a standing twist at the Celtic bench just a few feet away, felt his heart sink into an abyss.

The Celtics got a timeout with two seconds left, and the Lakers even left Bird open for a shot, which went in. But it didn't stay down, and Magic ran off happily, having stolen Game 4, 107-106.

Magic retired to the locker room to be lost in his eternal joy. He dubbed the shot "my junior, junior, junior sky hook."

"You expect to lose on a sky hook," Bird said with a sickly smile. "You don't expect it to be Magic."

Would the game be remembered just for its last minutes? Bird was asked. "It should," he replied. "A lot happened in the last minute-and-a-half. Robert gets the ball taken away from him. I throw the ball at Kevin's feet. They miss a free throw, and we don't get the rebound. How many chances do you need to win a game?"

Before Game 5, Bird told his teammates, "If they want to celebrate, let's not let them do it on the parquet." At one point during the contest, the Laker staff even iced down several cases of champagne. But the Celtics had incentive enough. They got their second win, 123-108, and the series jetted back across the continent.

The Celtics and Lakers managed one last fling in the 1987 championship series.

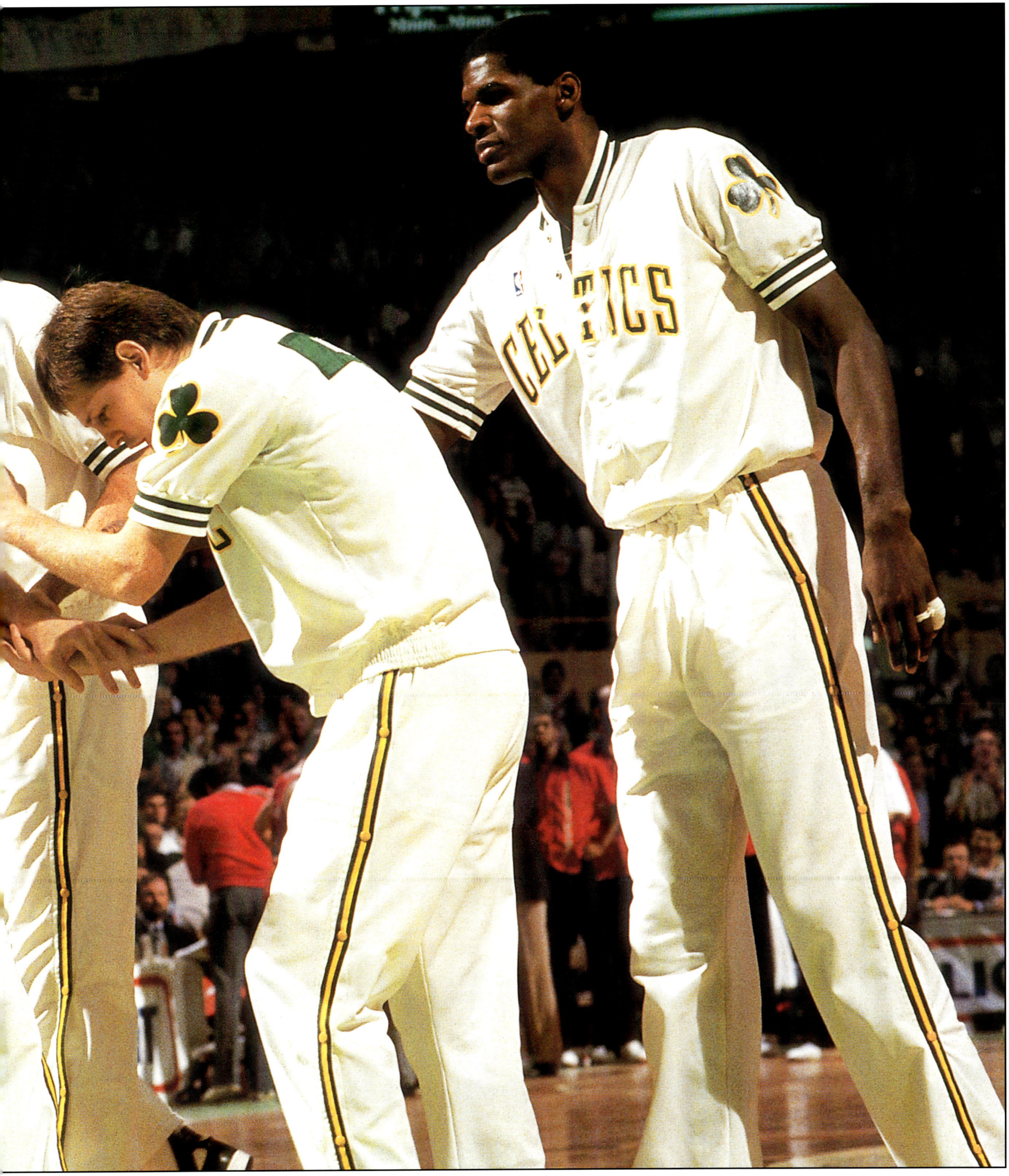

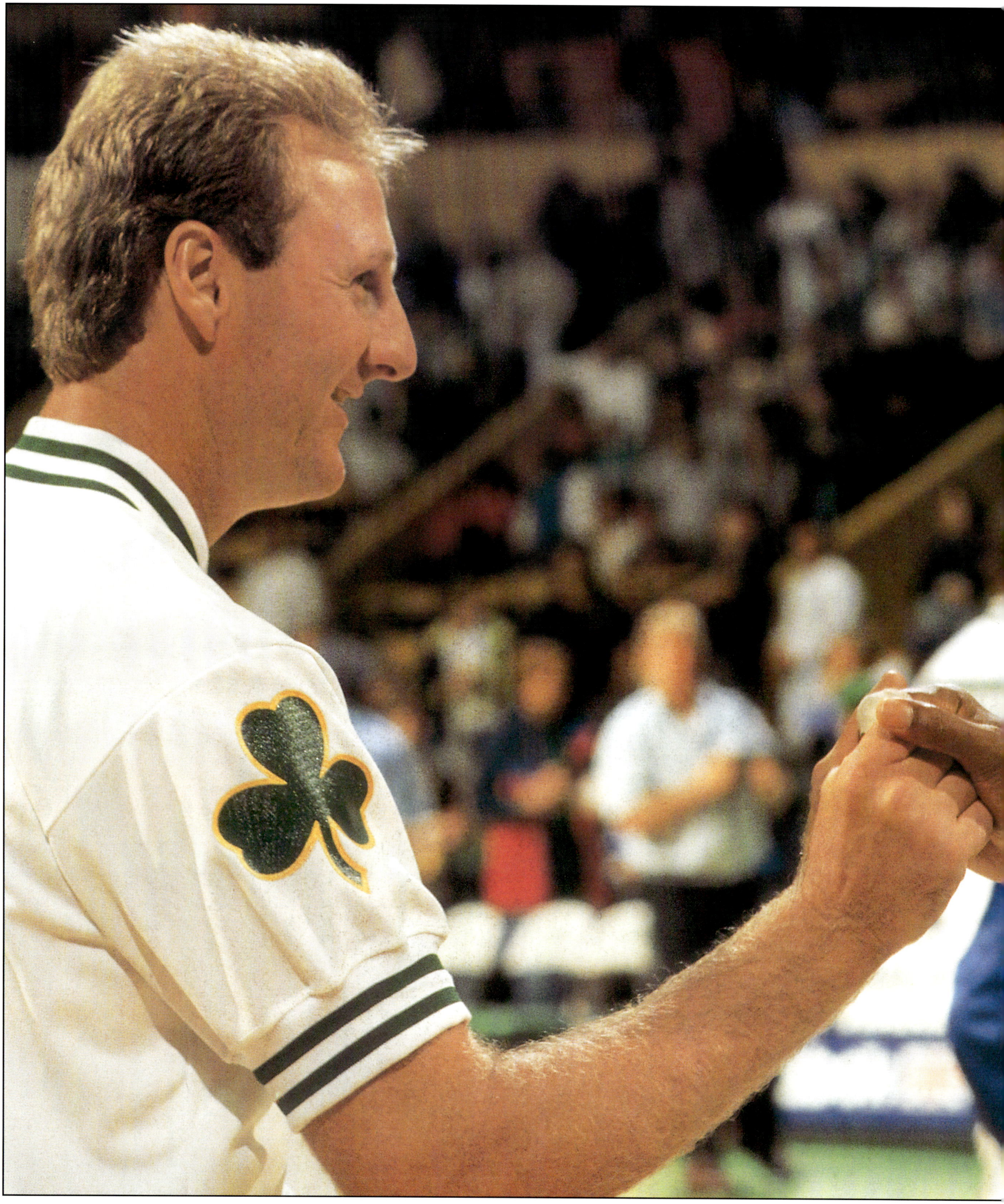

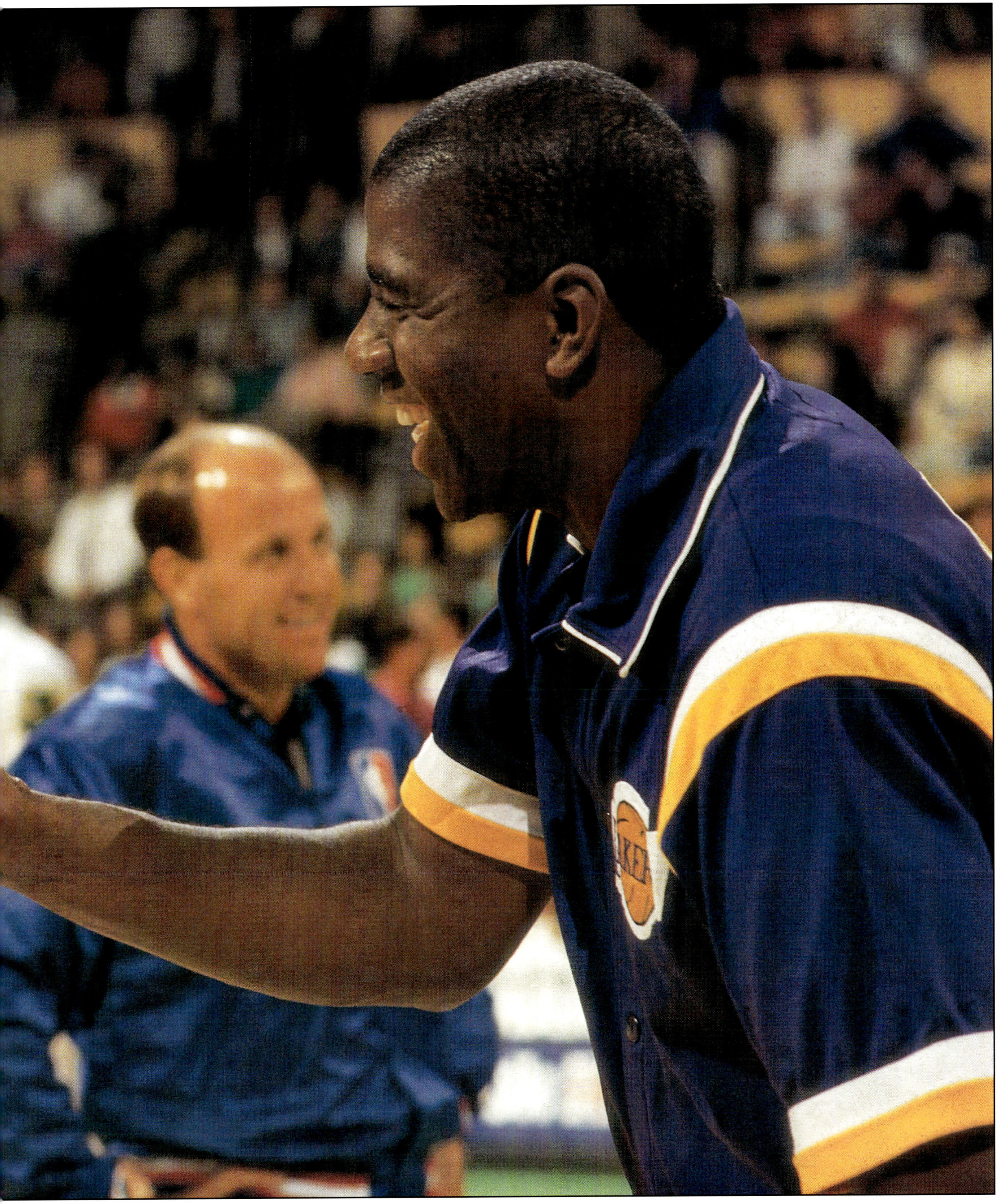

Kareem arrived for Game 6 with a shave job on his balding head. And for a time, it seemed Los Angeles was intent on cutting it close. Magic had only four points by the half, and the Celtics led, 56-51. But like Kareem's pate, the Lakers glistened after intermission. Worthy finished with 22, and Kareem had 32 points, six rebounds and four blocks. Mychal Thompson had 15 points and nine rebounds. And Magic led them with another performance of all-around brilliance. On top of his previous efforts, his 16-point, 19-assist, eight-rebound showing brought him the MVP award. And Los Angeles claimed their fourth title of the decade, 106-93.

"Magic is a great, great basketball player," Bird said. "The best I've ever seen."

Magic saw the reflection of his special talents in the team. "This is a super team, the best team I've played on," he said. "It's fast, they can shoot, rebound, we've got inside people, everything. I've never played on a team that had everything before. We've always had to play around something, but this team has it all."

Bird had to agree. "I guess this is the best team I've ever played against," he said. "In '85, they were good. In '84, I really thought they should have beaten us. . . I don't know if this team's better than they were, but I guess they are. Their fastbreak is better. They're deeper."

> "He was the smartest player I ever played against," Magic said of Bird. "I always enjoyed competing against him because he brought out the best in me. He was the only player that I truly feared."

Even with a healthy Bill Walton, the Celtics probably wouldn't have been able to alter the outcome, Bird said. "I would have loved to play them with a Bill Walton and a Scotty Wedman…. We would have given them a hell of a try."

The Lakers and Celtics had established a standard for pro basketball, and by 1987 they had begun to assume that the championship round was theirs to share.

Little did they know that their own private Camelot was slipping away.

The Celtics' injury problems would deepen over the ensuing seasons, as would the team's realization of just how big the Bias loss really was.

The years would pass, and Larry and Magic would never again meet in the Finals, with a championship on the line and the world watching.

Yet the spirit of their rivalry would come to rest at the very heart of pro basketball. And the intensity of all future rivalries would be measured against it.

"He was the smartest player I ever played against," Magic said of Bird. "I always enjoyed competing against him because he brought out the best in me. He was the only player that I truly feared."

SPORTS
KITE
KORNER
LAKERS
42
CELTICS
33
McHALE
LAKERS
45
NBA

BIRD: Portrait of a Competitor

Brothers In Arms

Larry. Kevin. Robert.

Bland as those three names are, they didn't require much of an introduction around the NBA during the Celtics' heydey in the 1980s.. Instead, they acquired their own collective nickname—The Big Three. For a dozen special seasons, they performed roundball miracles on the Garden parquet together. It was a thrilling time for Boston crowds, who spent the best months of each year watching Bird, Parish and McHale put together sequence after sequence of spectacular plays. The spectacular, in fact, became almost commonplace.

"They are the greatest front line since the NBA was formed," Celtics president Red Auerbach once boasted between puffs of his cigar.

Better than Mikan, Mikkelsen and Pollard.

Better than Reed, DeBusschere and Bradley.

Better than Kareem, Worthy and Green.

Better than Russell, Heinsohn and Ramsey.

Better than Cowens, Havlicek and Silas.

Better than Erving, Malone and Jones.

Better than Walton, Lucas and Gross.

Better than Pettit, Macauley and Hagan.

And certainly better than Laimbeer, Rodman and Edwards.

Asked to come up with a frontcourt to match The Big Three, Hall of Famer Rick Barry suggested the 1967 Philadelphia trio of Wilt Chamberlain, Lucious Jackson and Billy Cunningham.

"That would be the only frontcourt that could come close to comparing to them," he said.

But even they couldn't matchup with the Boston's great ones, Barry added.

Besides, Wilt, Jackson and Cunningham only played together two full seasons.

Larry, Robert and Kevin were together for nearly a fourth of the NBA's entire history.

"Those guys have gone through everything you can go through," Celtic Dee Brown observed. "They've been through so much and found every which way to win."

Their three NBA championships and five conference titles stand as a testament to that. It's also their ticket to a first-ballot entry into the Hall of Fame.

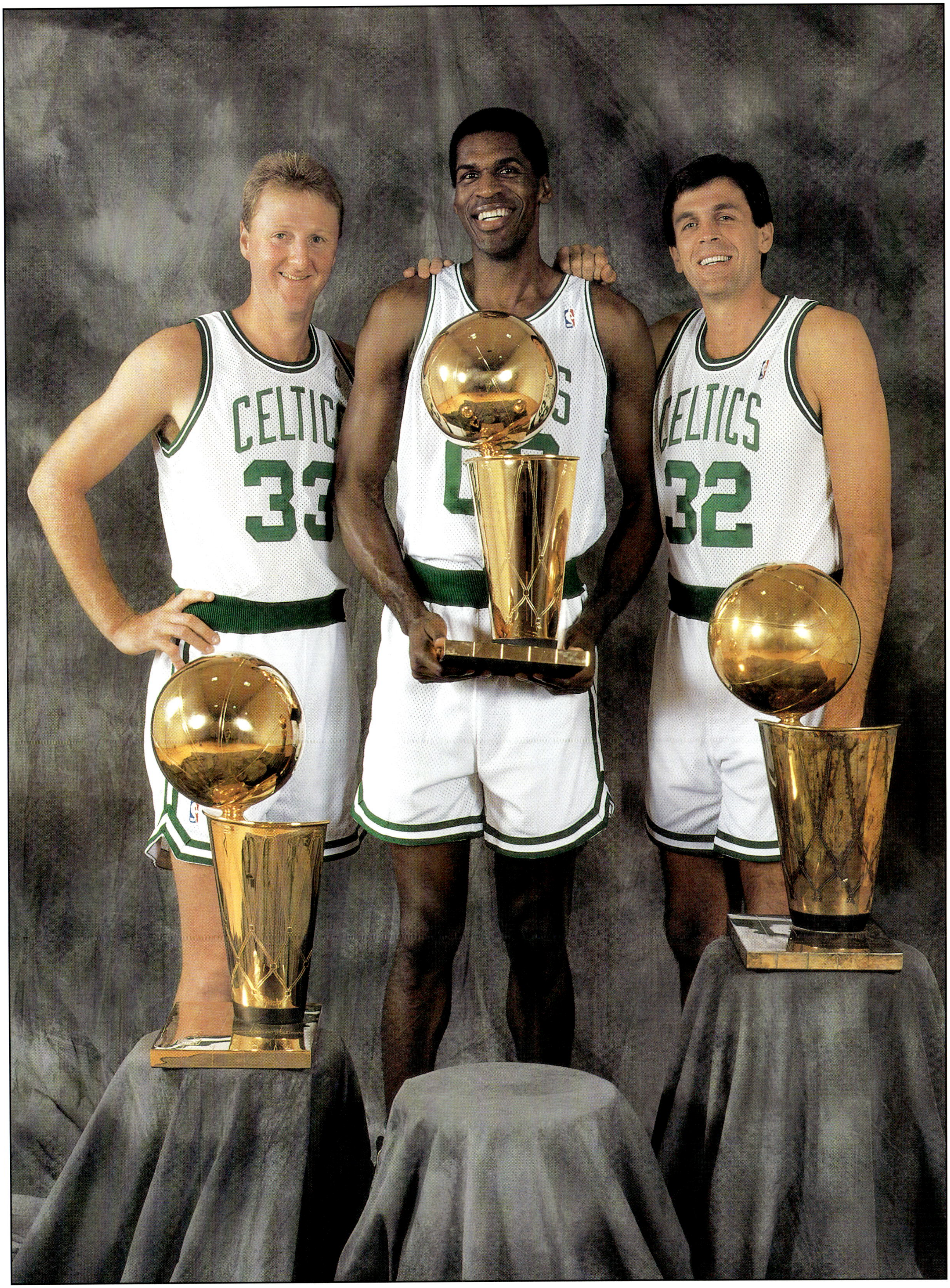
CELTICS
33
32

The Big Three with Dennis Johnson and Danny Ainge.

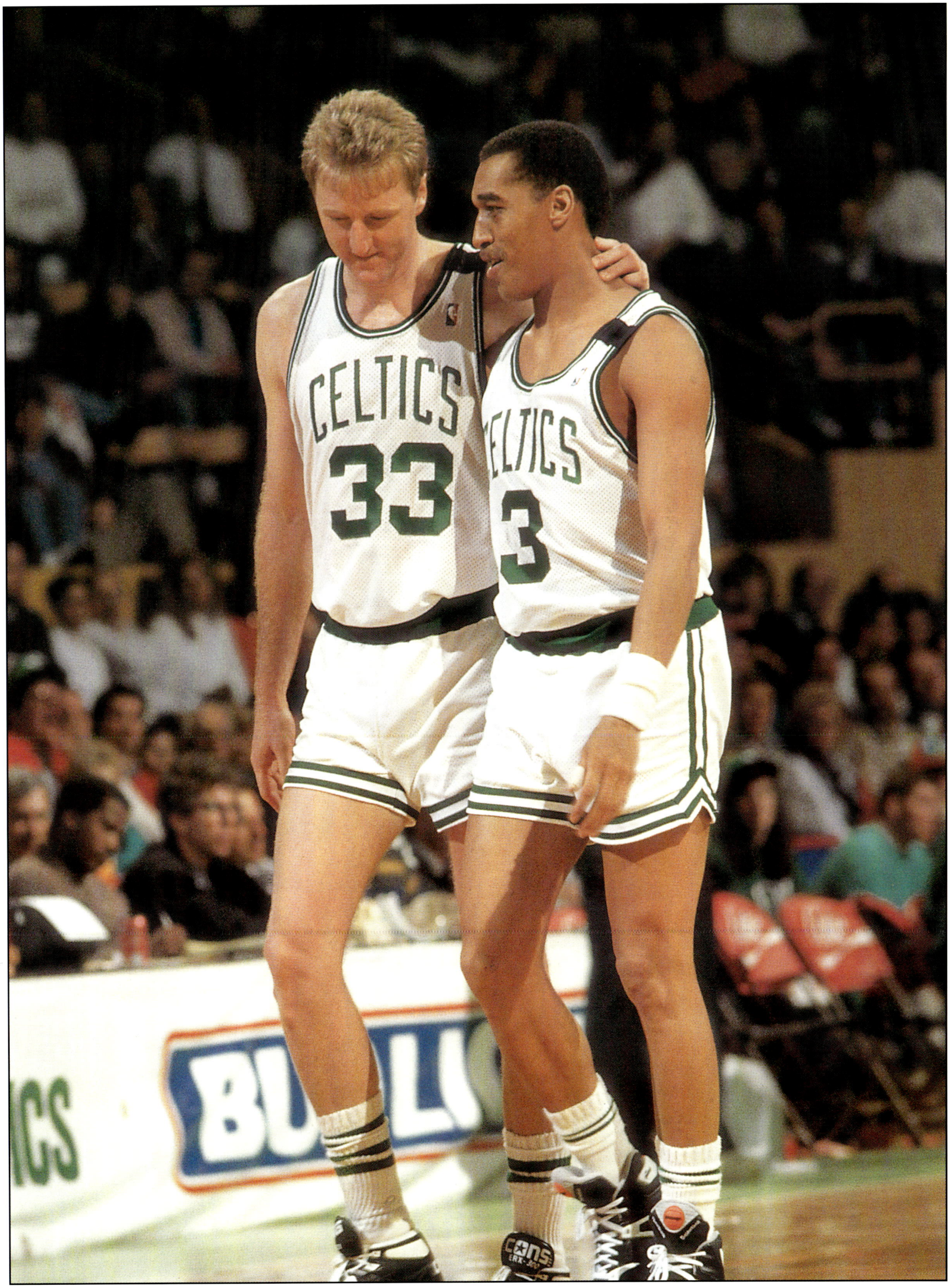
CELTICS
33

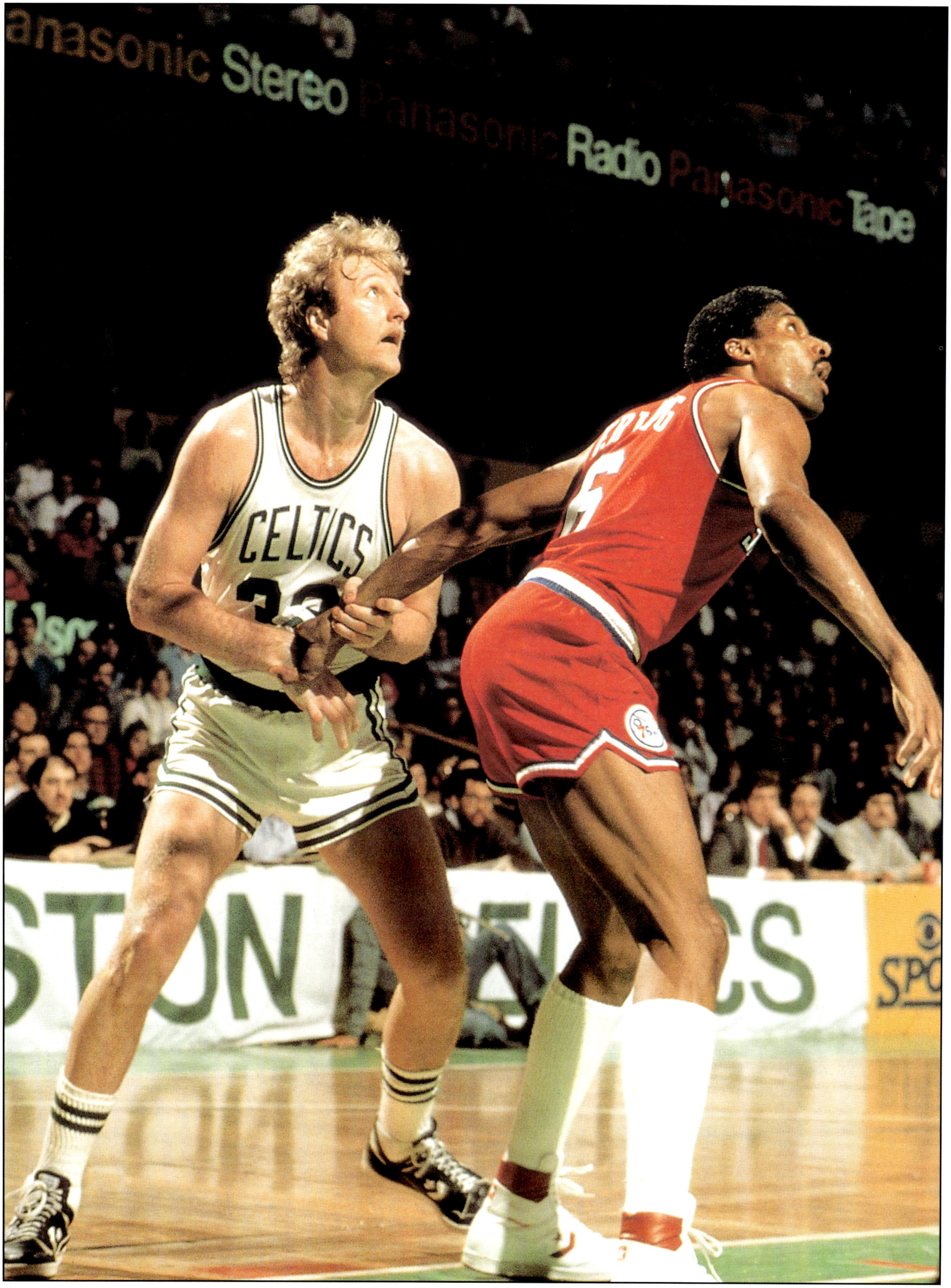
anasonic Stereo Panasonic Radio Panasonic Tape
CELTICS

III Nemeses

Dominique Wilkins likes to tell a story from his rookie season in 1982, when he met Bird for the first time and attempted to shake hands before a game. Bird ignored the extended hand and answered only with a cold stare. In that single moment, Wilkins learned what most players around the league already knew: Bird was an uncompromising competitor. "Look in his eyes," Wilkins later said, "and you see a killer."

James Worthy of the Lakers openly despised Bird. "Larry would always say, 'Get down!' or 'In your face!' or 'You can't guard me!'," Worthy recalled. "Whatever he could use to throw you off balance, that was his biggest weapon over the years. Back then, when I was young and didn't know any better, I thought he was a jerk. But after reflecting back, I realized that was just part of his game. He was measuring and analyzing his opponents, and he would do it from the moment he stepped on the floor. In the layup line, he'd be looking down there at you, just checking out your tendencies and your mannerisms and your posture. He could tell if your confidence wasn't right. He could tell. He could sense the vibe. If you came out on him and really didn't bump him or weren't aggressive with him, he knew. He knew he had you. If you showed any signs of doubt, you were through with Larry."

From Philadelphia's Julius Erving, who ended up in an angry, violent tussle with Bird one night after listening to too much of Larry's trash talk, to Detroit's Isiah Thomas, who endured years of frustration losing to the Celtics, opponents around the league held a grudging respect for Bird tempered by one fact: Nobody liked losing to him, least of all his ultimate foe, Earvin "Magic" Johnson.

The fact that Bird was white and most of his top foes were black also factored into the equation. Without doubt, there were sportswriters (this author included) who unconsciously became fans of Bird because, in part, of his race. This admiration was frequently reflected in the reporting about Bird's feats and accomplishments. The situation boiled over in the 1987 playoffs, after Boston had defeated the Detroit Pistons, when a frustrated Dennis Rodman lashed out that Bird was overemphasized by the media because he was white. Isiah Thomas, Rodman's Detroit teammate, agreed, saying that if Bird were black, he'd be considered just another good player. The remarks

BIRD: Portrait of a Competitor

brought a firestorm of criticism in the press, and Bird was understandably hurt. But he sat with Thomas in an ensuing press conference during which the Detroit guard attempted to explain his remarks as being critical of the media, not of Bird's abilities.

Perhaps the highest praise for Bird came from his keenest competitor, Michael Cooper, the sixth man on the Los Angeles Lakers' great teams in the 1980s and a defensive whiz. He built his reputation playing Bird tough and was obsessed with defending Larry. "Larry Bird is what they call the ultimate basketball player," Cooper once offered. No one would have known that better than Cooper. He had a complete video library of Bird and spent his spare time, even a 1987 European vacation, studying Larry's moves.

Bird, likewise, was a serious student of his opponents and could offer precise evaluations of their abilities. For example, Michael Jordan, a rookie during the 1984-85 season, scored 27 points in an early loss to the Celtics in Chicago Stadium. It was his first meeting with a Bird-led team. "I've never seen one player turn a team around like that," Larry, the league's reigning Most Valuable Player, said afterward. "All the Bulls have become better because of him. . . . Pretty soon this place will be packed every night. . . . They'll pay just to watch Jordan. He's the best. Even at this stage in his career, he's doing more than I ever did. I couldn't do what he does as a rookie. Heck, there was one drive tonight. He had the ball up in his right hand, then he took it down. Then he brought it back up. I got a hand on it, fouled him, and he still scored. All the while, he's in the air.

"You have to play this game to know how difficult that is. You see that and say, 'Well, what the heck can you do?' I'd seen a little of him before and wasn't that impressed. I mean, I thought he'd be good, but not this good. Ain't nothing he can't do. That's good for this franchise, good for the league."

Bird, for the most part, was also brutally honest in comparing his abilities with those he faced. Nothing bore that out any more than the events that closed the 1988 season, as ultimately disappointing as they were for Boston fans. Bird continued his stellar play and seemed a favorite to claim his fourth league MVP award. But as the award came down to a vote, a controversy stewed. Chicago's Michael Jordan had turned in an incredible offensive and defensive year, becoming the first player to lead the league in both scoring and steals, and various writers and observers took turns stating why Bird or Jordan deserved the nod. At the crucial juncture before the voting, Bird spoke out and said Jordan deserved the award (the Chicago guard later won). Bird didn't offer that opinion as an attempt at false modesty, but simply because he had become convinced Jordan had put together a better season.

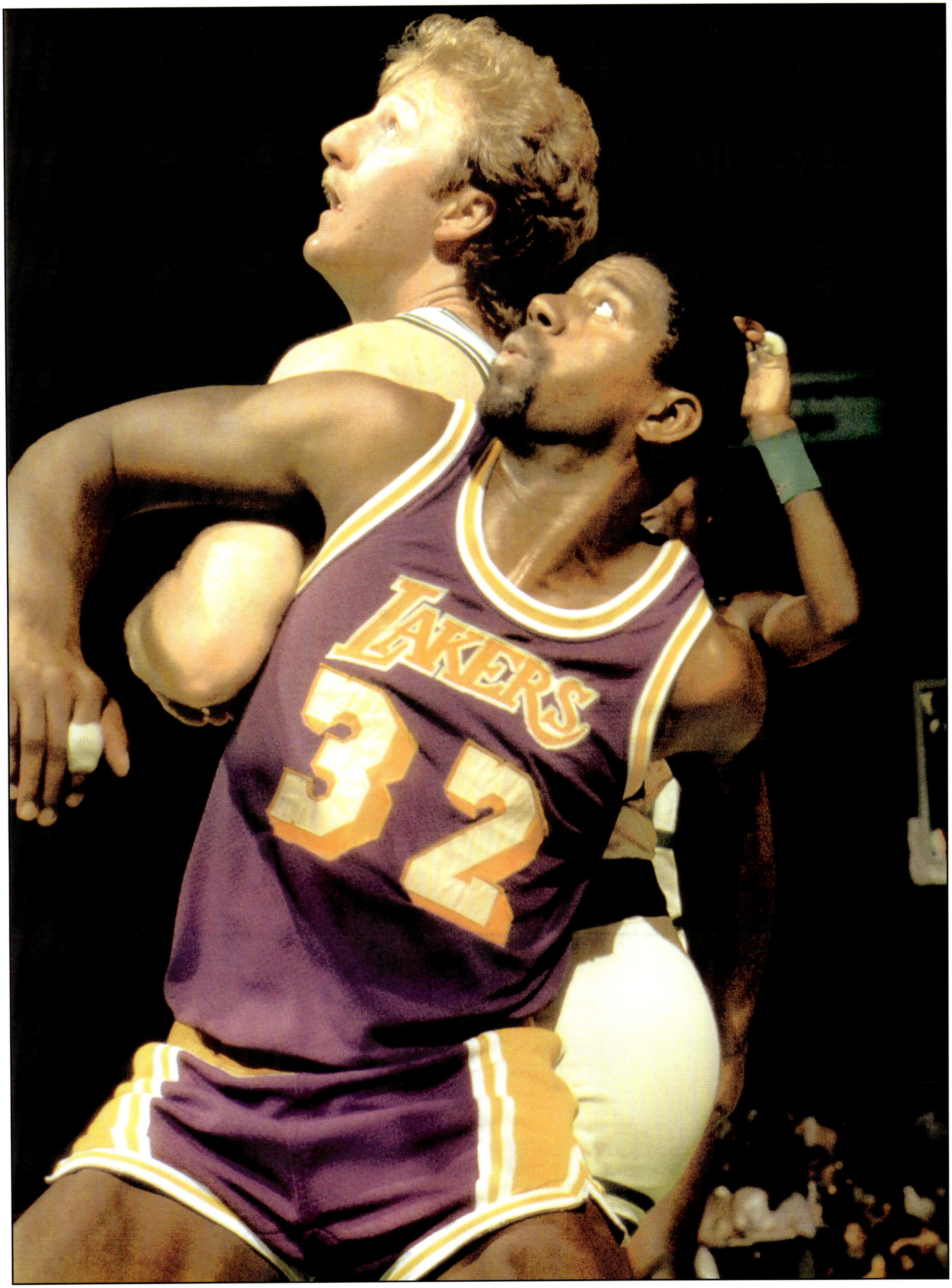
LAKERS
32

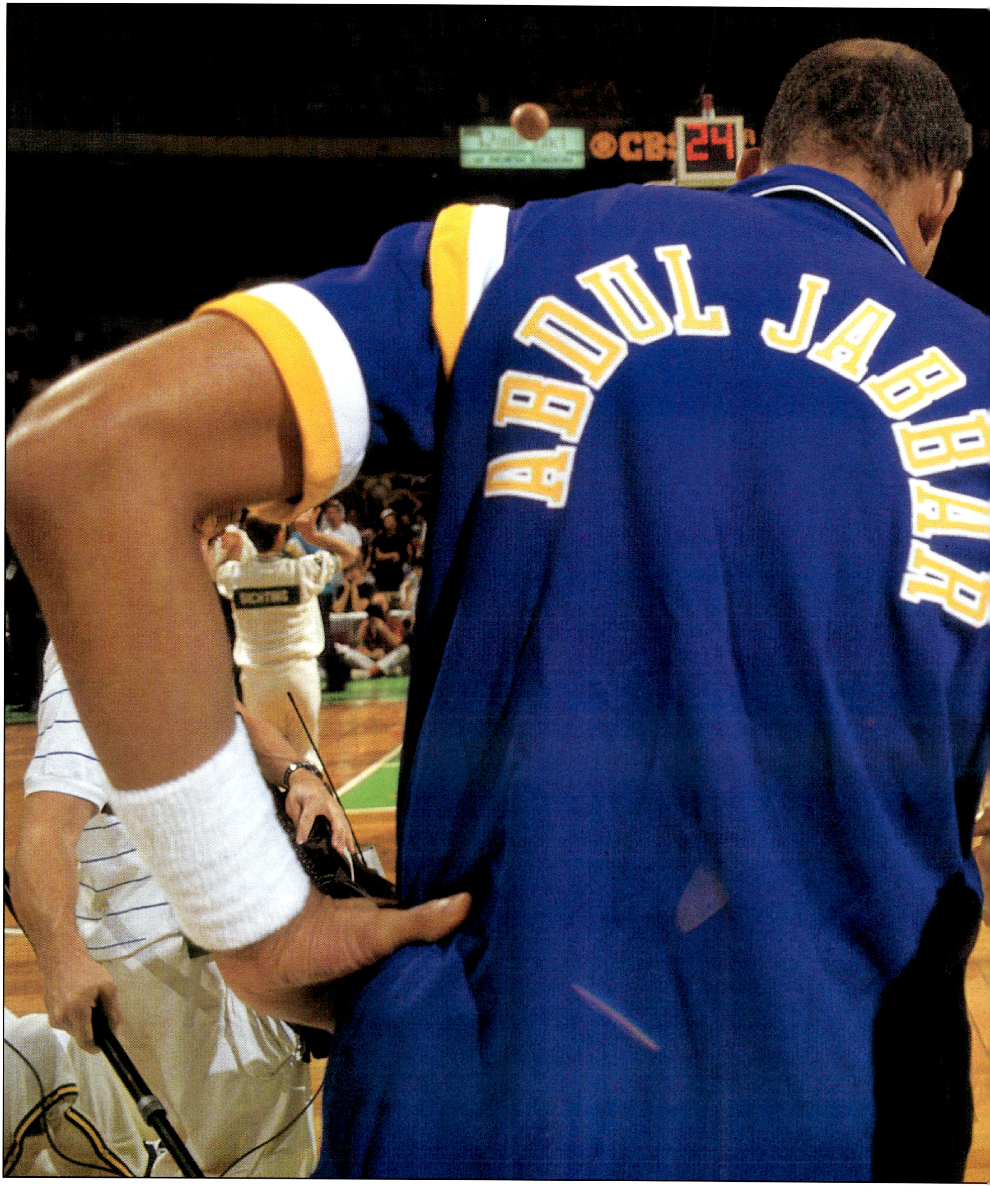
ABDUL JABBAR
CBS
24

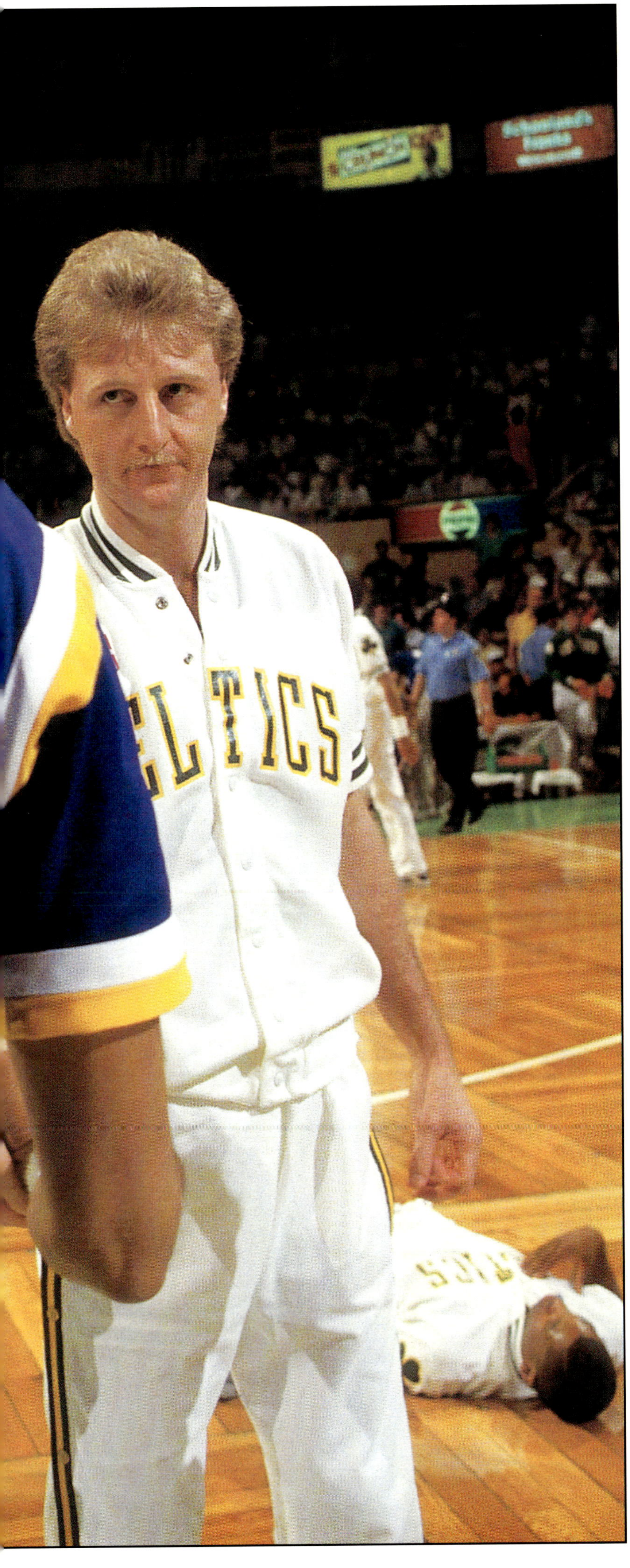
ELTICS

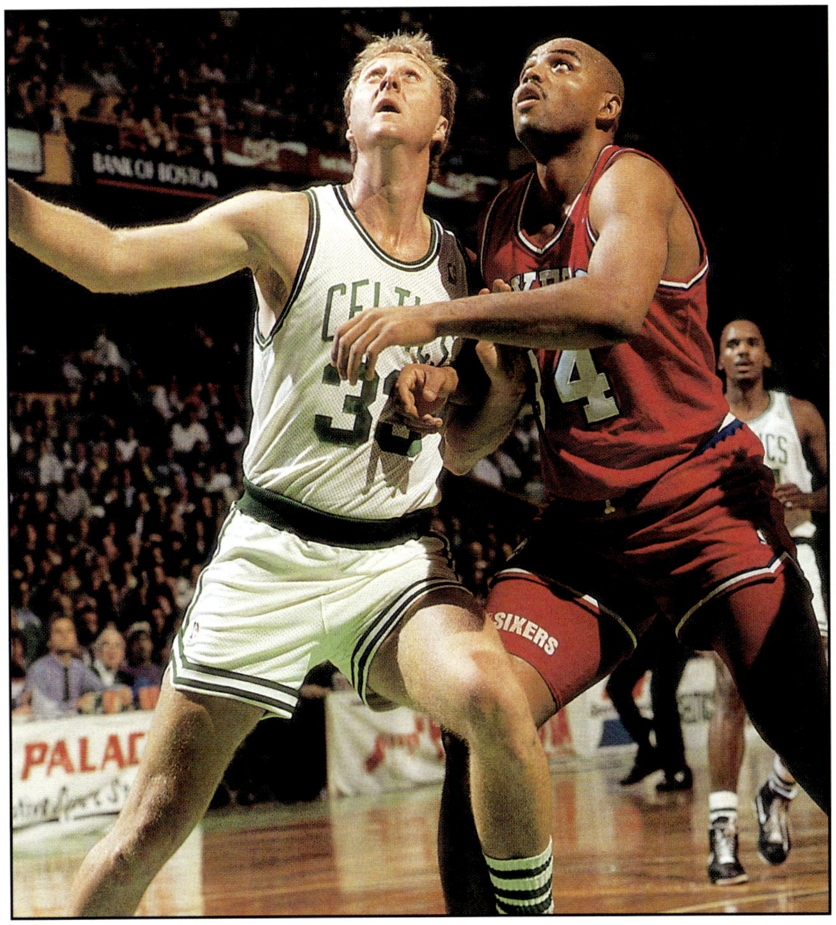
BANK OF BOSTON
SIXERS

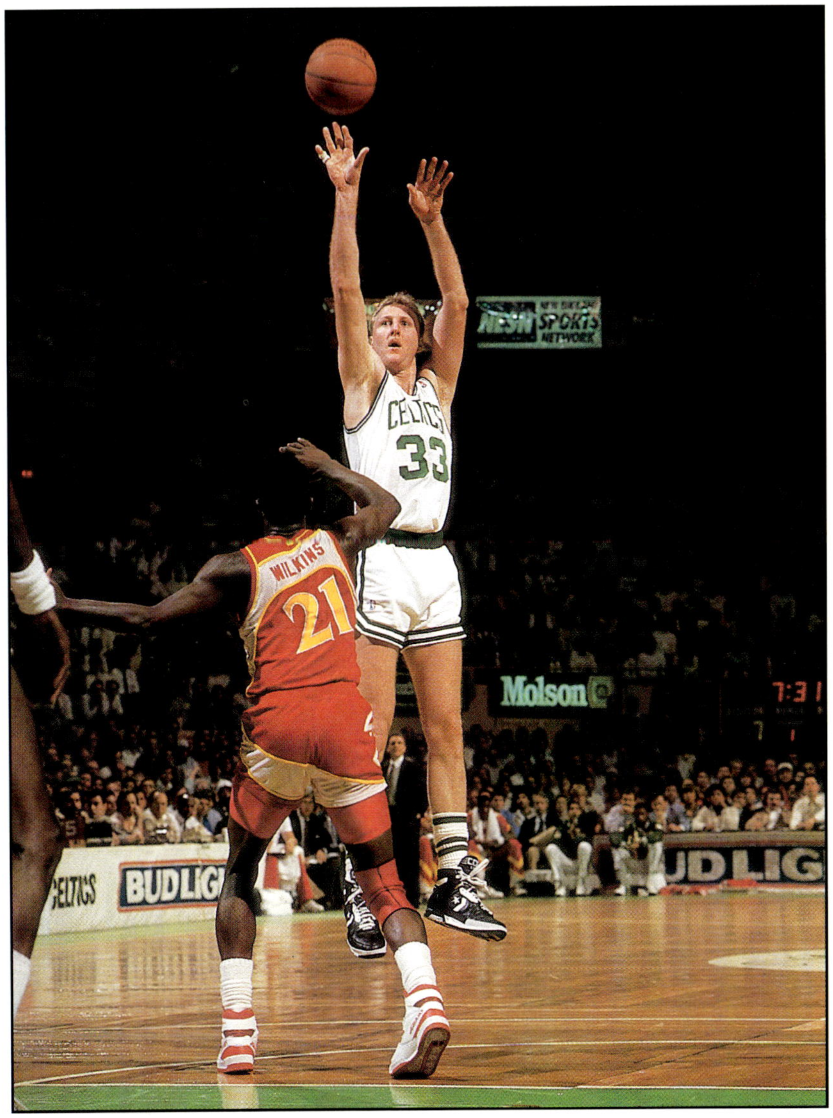
CELTICS
33
WILKINS
21
Molson

" If he were black, he'd be just another good guy." - Isiah Thomas. Larry rescued Isiah after the firestorm of controversy surrounding Isiah's comment.

" I think he's way overrated... He can't run. He's slow." - Dennis Rodman.

Michael Cooper was his toughest defender, Bird said.

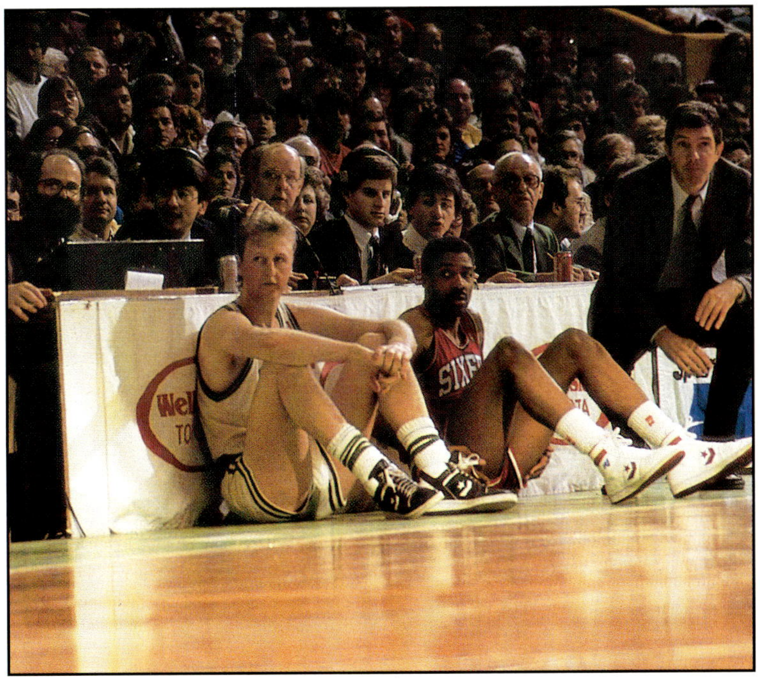

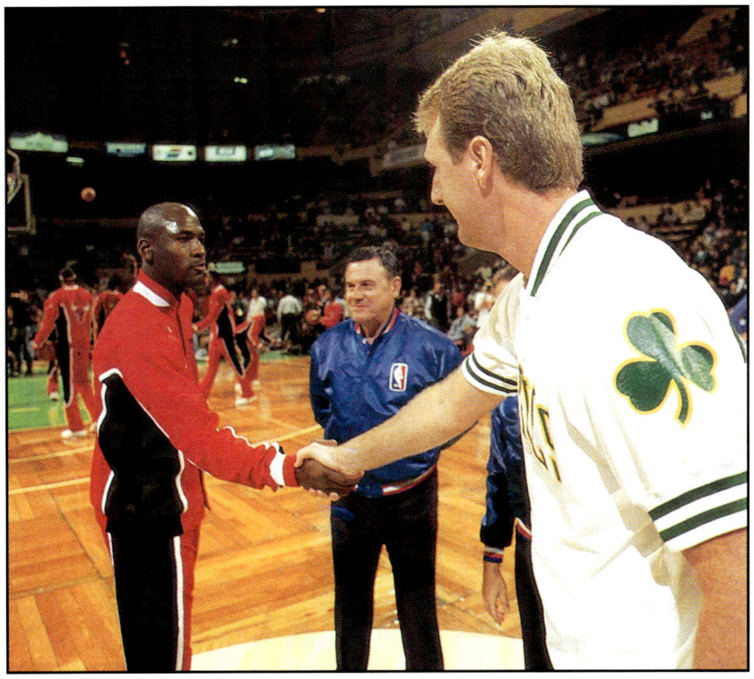

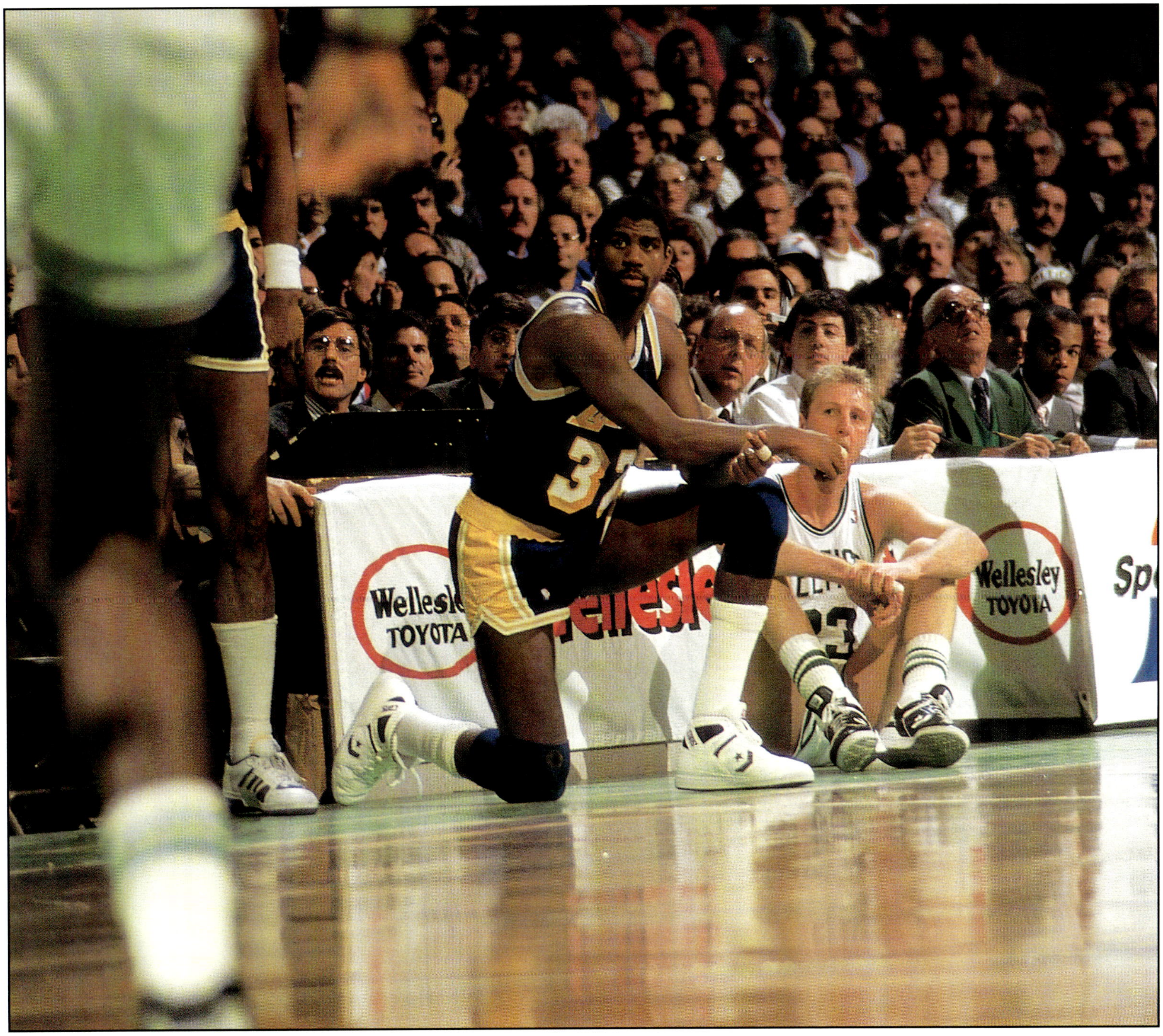
Wellesley TOYOTA
Wellesley TOYOTA

Playing with Pain
IV

With a playing style that emphasized throwing himself into impossible situations and sacrificing his body to make plays, it's no wonder that Bird was troubled by injury and pain throughout his career. His back. His elbows. His Achilles tendons. The grind of competing at the furtherest recesses of desire took a toll on his body and meant the eventual deterioration of his game.

It was a process that began with his first days as a Celtic.

Bird had shattered his right index finger catching a line drive in a softball game the spring of his senior year at Indiana State, which led to even more questions about his adjustment to the pros. He answered them by altering his shot to compensate for the injury, and although the injured digit was taped to his middle finger, he established a presence in training camp that fall.

The cumulative effect of hundreds of NBA battles over the next seven seasons took their toll. When the Celtics lost to the Lakers in the 1987 NBA Finals, Larry knew he had to take a proactive approach to his body. The loss became the fuel for Bird's new burst of motivation. He went back home to Indiana and began an exercise routine that included hill and road work, stationary cycling, jumping rope, weightlifting and stretching for two hours per day, five days a week. Bird also trimmed his long blond hair to reflect his businesslike approach. He reported to training camp that fall 15 pounds lighter and obviously much stronger. "After last season," he told reporters, "I was really fatigued. When the season was over, I was glad. I had never felt that way before. I also thought the weights would strengthen my back and elbow, which I'd had problems with. I wanted to come back strong, and felt that if I lost weight, and did some work with free weights, that I'd be stronger at the end of the season than I was last year."

Although McHale was out with a foot injury, Bird opened the 1987-88 season with an All-Star determination, shifted some emphasis to low-post scoring and helped take up the slack. On November 7th, he scored 47 points and the winning bucket in double overtime to beat Washington. Four days later he scored 42 points and had 20 rebounds in a win over Indiana, the first time in Celtic history a player had scored more than 40 and rebounded for 20 in the same game. That pace continued until a week later when he injured both Achilles tendons in a loss to the Cavaliers. He missed five games but rebuilt his momentum until just after the February All Star game, when his eye socket was shattered by a Dell Curry elbow in another meeting with Cleveland. Wearing protective goggles, he returned to the lineup and resumed his pace.

That was how he responded to injury, seeking to find some way around it to keep competing. But by the 1988-89 season, he was hobbled by spurs on his heels and had no solution but surgery. He played briefly to start the season but soon made his decision. The result was a yearlong convalescence. Even when he returned it was obvious that the injuries had taken their toll, that Bird had reached the apex of his career and was now headed downhill.

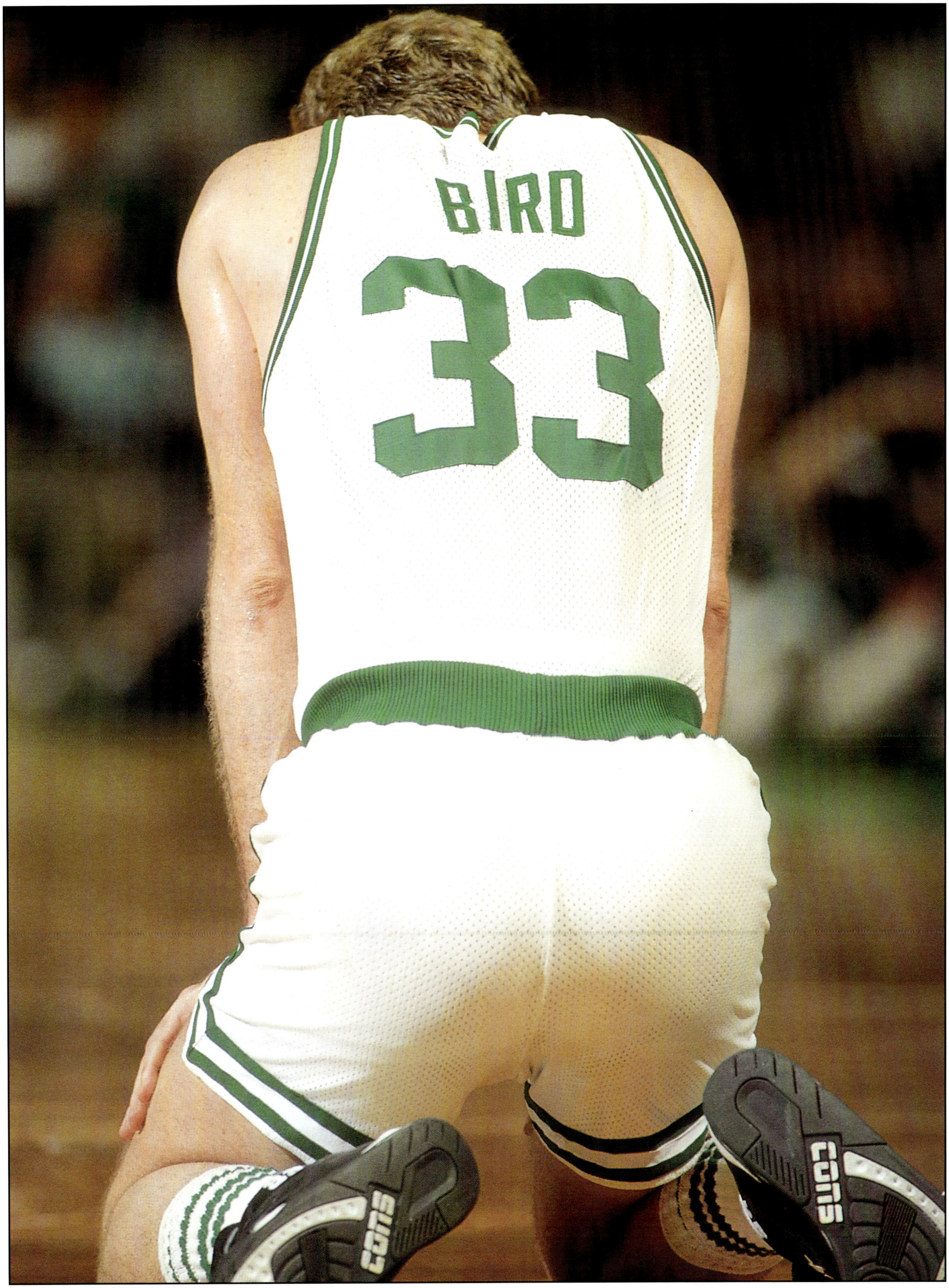
BIRD
33
cons
cons

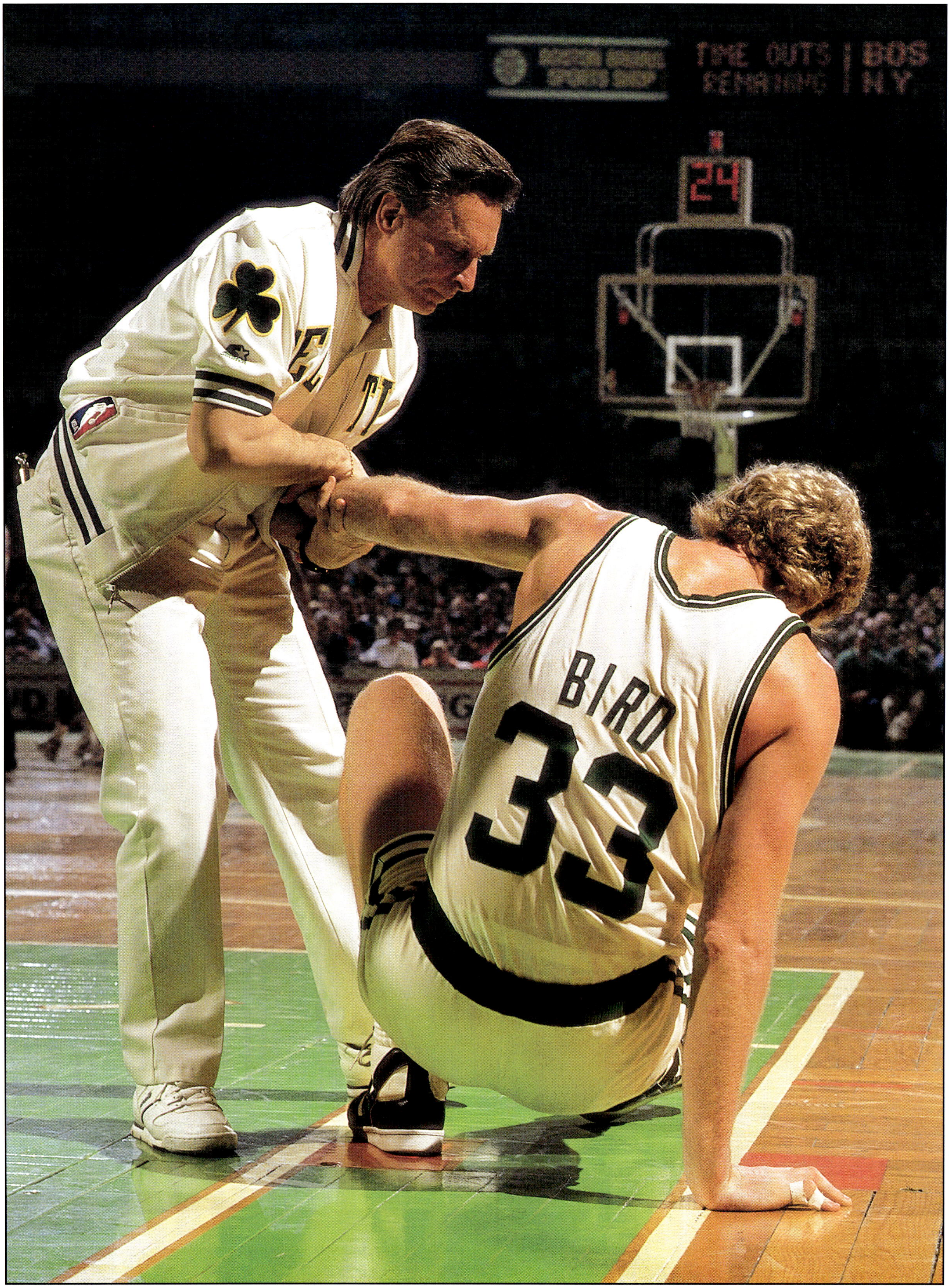
TIME OUTS
BOS
N.Y.
24
BIRD
33

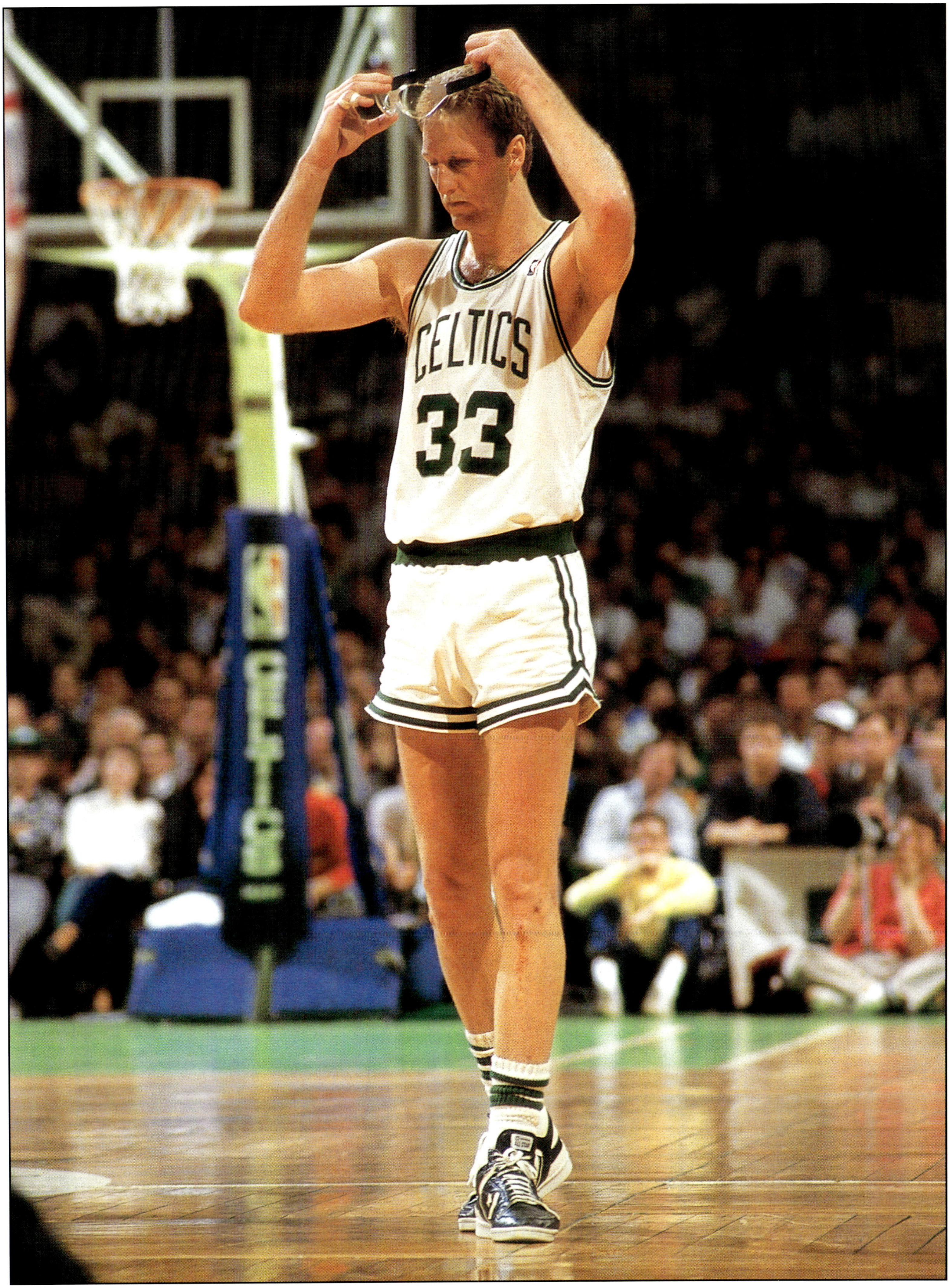
CELTICS
33
CELTICS

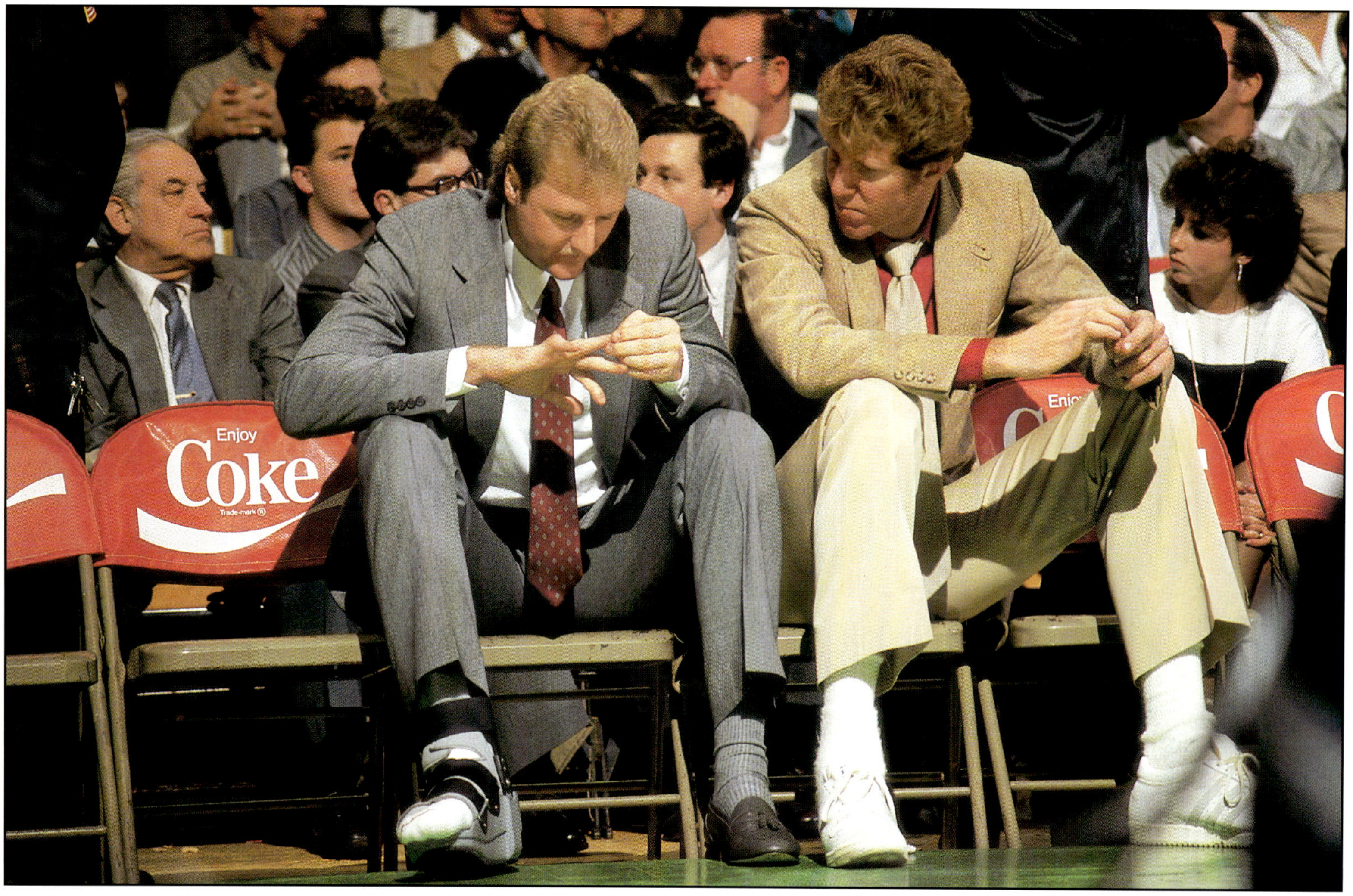
Enjoy
Coke

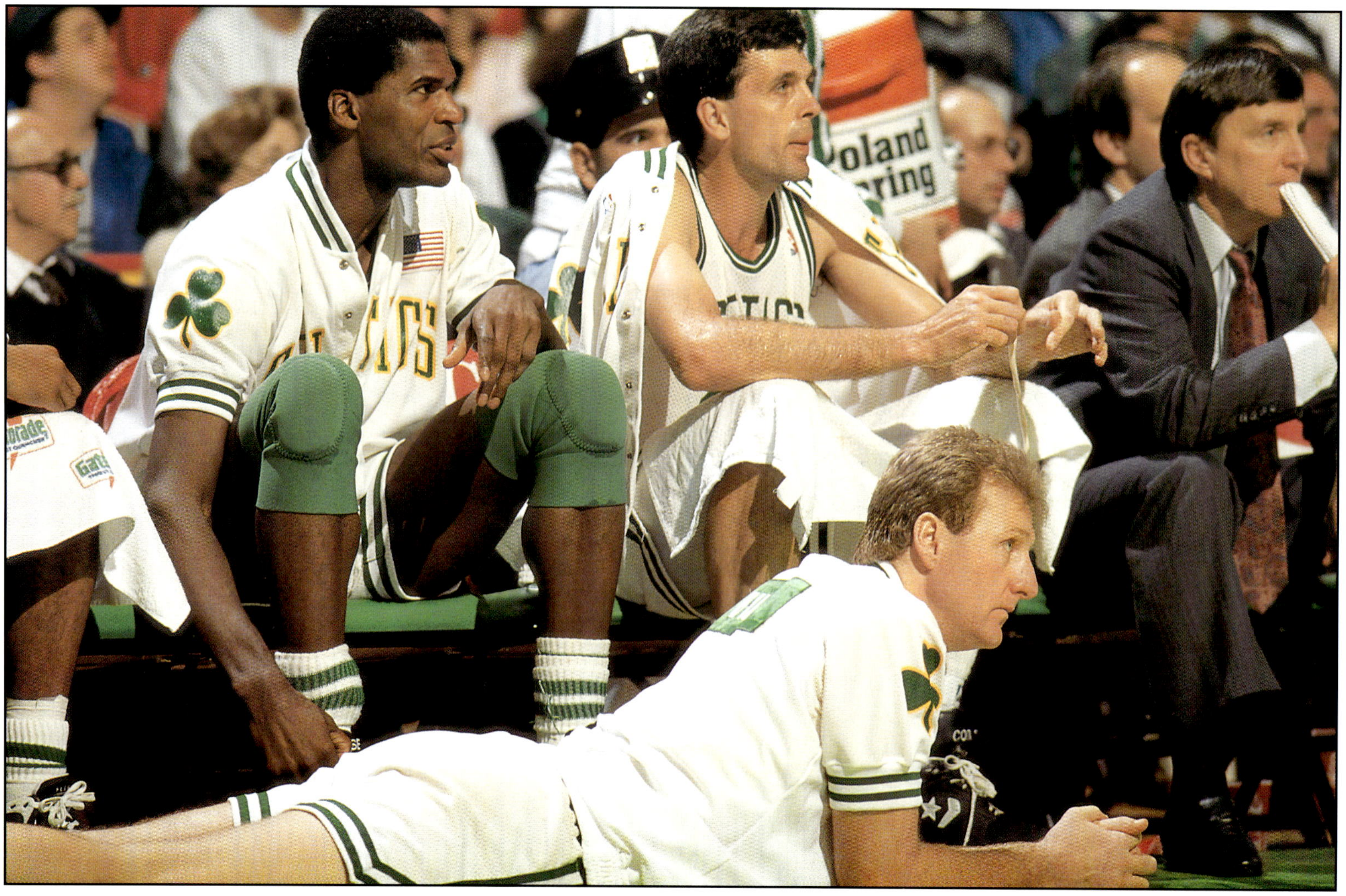

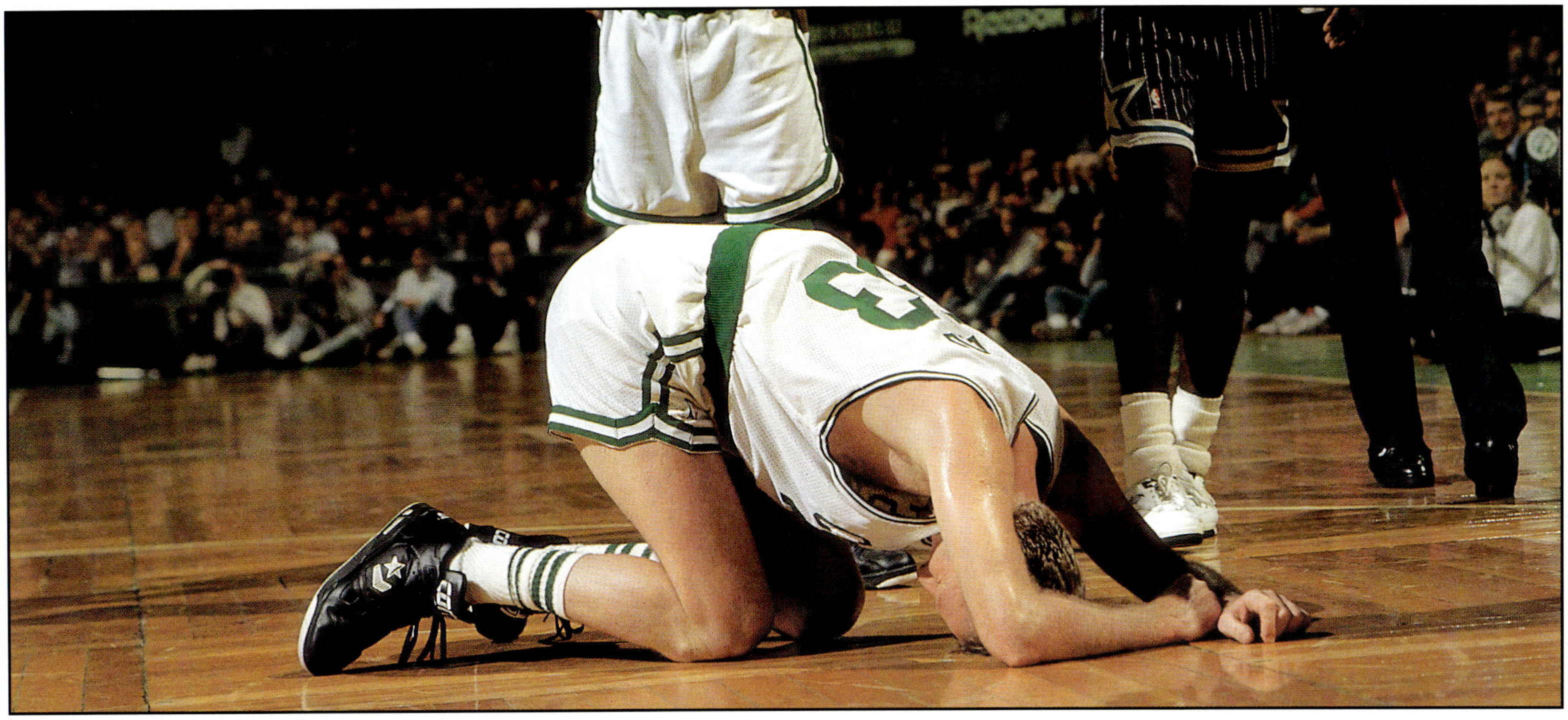
Reebok

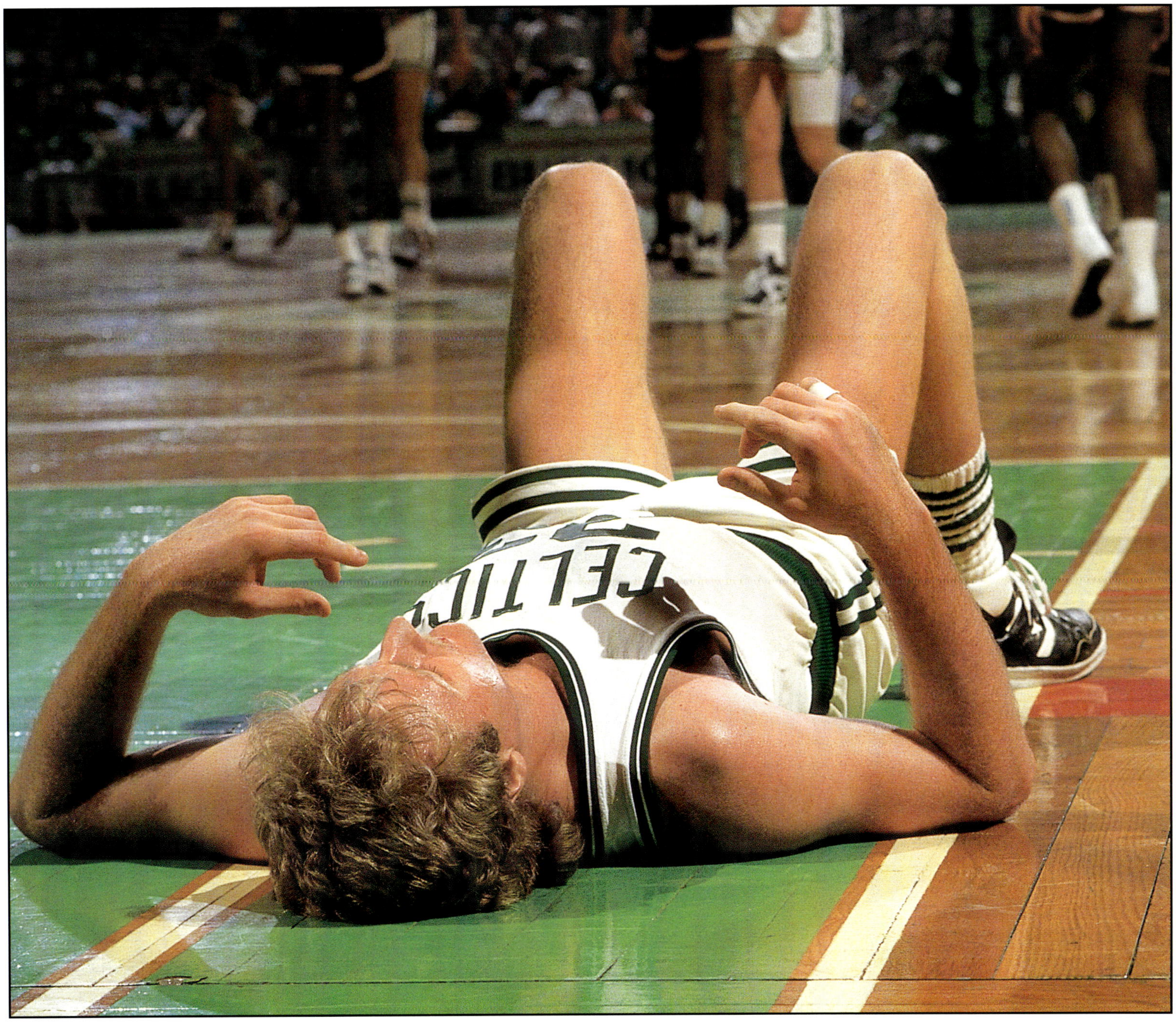
CELTICS

His return from every injury was something the fans anticipated.

BOSTON CELTICS 1969 WORLD CHAMPIONS
BOSTON CELTICS 1968 WORLD CHAMPIONS
BOSTON CELTICS 1960 WORLD CHAMPIONS
BOSTON CELTICS 1959 WORLD CHAMPIONS
BOSTON CELTICS 1957 WORLD CHAMPIONS
BIRD'S BACK
GET THE WHOLE PICTURE...ON
BIRD'S BACK
GET THE WHOLE PICTURE...ON

V Letting Go

In retrospect, it was one of those rare situations where the legend couldn't outlast the reality. The legend, of course, was Larry. And the reality was his aching, 35-year-old back, which finally forced him to announce his retirement August 18, 1992, ending speculation on whether he would attempt to return to the Boston Celtics for a 14th season.

"If I was healthy this year and I knew I could have helped my team, I would've played," Bird told a hastily arranged news conference at Boston Garden. "But the injuries got a hold of me and I couldn't shake 'em."

The announcement came as no great surprise—Bird had fought to overcome a variety of injuries over the past four years. But the moment still carried plenty of attendant emotion. His retirement and the on-again, off-again plans of Earvin Johnson, Jr., Bird's friend and longtime foe with the Los Angeles Lakers, brought to a close a glorious era in the history of basketball.

"I think Robert Parish was the best teammate I ever played with, and Dennis Johnson was the best player I ever played with," Bird said in praising his band of Celtic brothers. "M.L. Carr was probably the funniest teammate I ever had, and Kevin McHale was the best inside player I've ever seen."

Until Bird and Johnson came along in the fall of 1979, the game had struggled to find an identity among American professional sports. But Larry and Earvin changed all that. The public had never quite seen anything like their rivalry. Larry and the Celtics vs. Magic and the Lakers. By 1986, the two had led their teams to three NBA championships apiece, and suddenly the whole world was interested. Or so it seemed.

They could play, those Celtics and Lakers.

At one time or another, Magic had Kareem Abdul-Jabbar, Jamaal Wilkes, James Worthy, Robert McAdoo, Norm Nixon and Michael Cooper alongside him. Bird's Celtics featured Kevin McHale, the Chief, Dennis Johnson, Tiny Archibald, M.L. Carr, Cedric Maxwell, Dave Cowens, Bill Walton and Danny Ainge.

If Bird was their king, Boston Garden was his castle. "Hell," he once quipped, "this is my building."

It wasn't easy for Larry to turn loose his grip on greatness.

His wife, Dinah, had suggested retirement a year earlier. But he persisted, hoping that the back pain would go away. Over the summer, retirement "was in and out of my head," he said. After the Olympic Games ended in early August, his deliberations intensified. He spent late nights twisting and turning, trying to decide.

There was hope that he might try to play a 60-game schedule that would diminish his travel. Never a part-time guy, he quickly nixed that option.

"That's not the way I approach things," he explained.

Finally he faced the inevitable, spoke with his doctors and made up his mind.

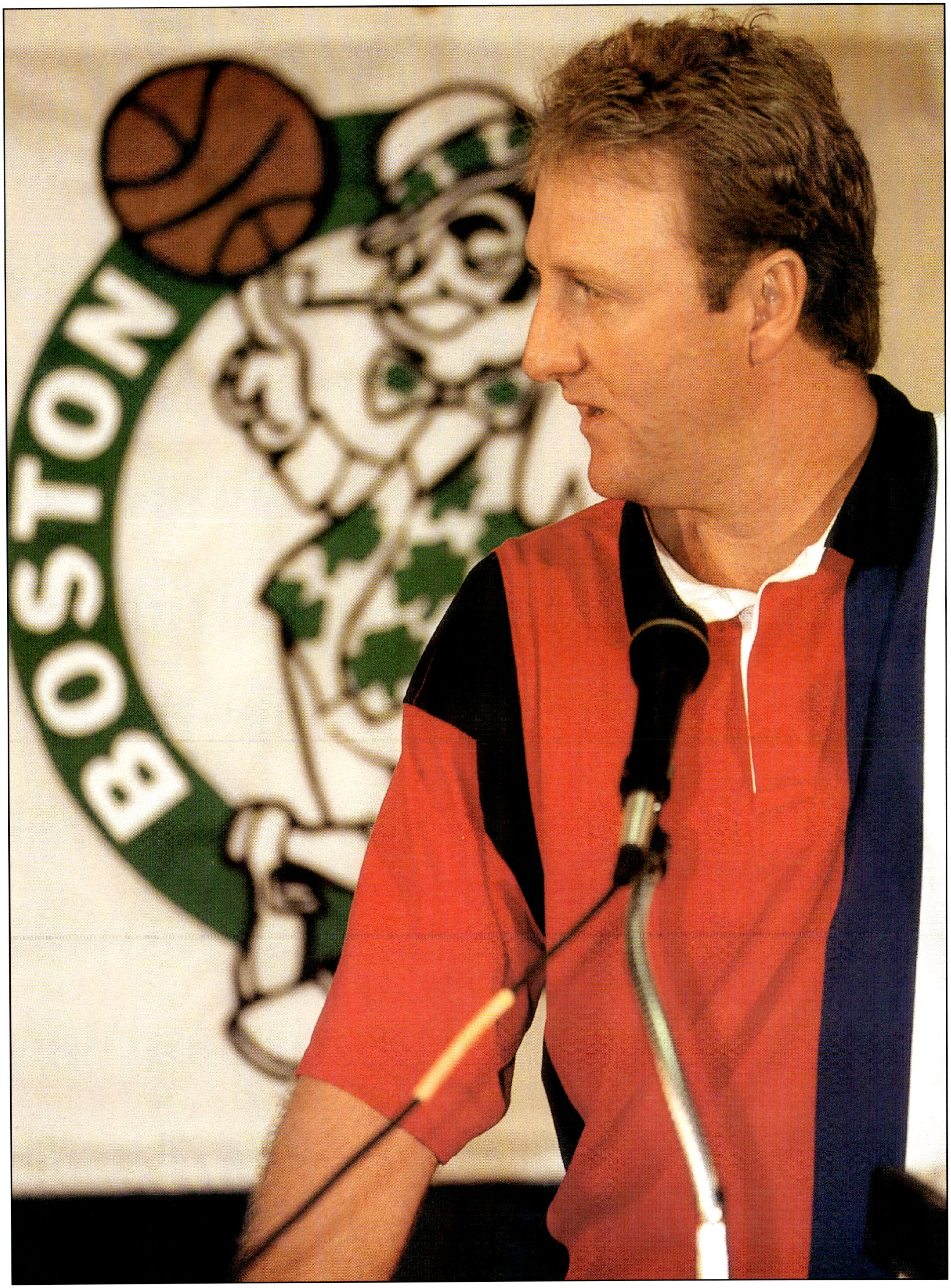
BOSTON

BIRD: Portrait of a Competitor

"Are you sure?" Celtics executive Dave Gavitt asked when Bird informed him of his decision.

He was sure.

"Emotionally, it's very tough for me right now because I'm giving up something I love, something I have been doing for a long time," he said in announcing his retirement. "But I have to give it up. I don't want to go out this way, but I have to."

Despite the sadness, the press conference was not a time of gloom for Red Auerbach. Rather, it was a time to celebrate the accomplishments of a great basketball club. Auerbach had constructed three great teams in Boston—the Bill Russell dynasty, the Dave Cowens group and Bird's teams. So Red wasn't just saying goodbye to Larry, he was saying goodbye to a part of himself.

He stepped up first and offered the perspective of his 42 years with what is arguably America's greatest pro sports club. ("If you never played for the Boston Celtics, you never really played professional basketball," Bird said.)

"I remember when he first came here," Auerbach told the assembly. "He looked like a country bumpkin. But when you looked in his eyes, you knew he was no dummy."

Yet Auerbach admitted that even Bird's eyes didn't reveal just how good he was going to be.

The press asked Bird when he himself knew he was headed for greatness. "It didn't take me long to realize I was going to be a great player in this league," he answered. "I remember the day of rookie camp down in Marshfield. Dave Cowens was there, and Tiny Archibald, and M.L. Carr. It seemed that everyone showed up to see how good I was going to be. The thing is, Rick Robey was covering me, so I thought I was going to be even better than I was."

The laughter rolled through the room, but the media suspected he was masking his feelings.

Bird was asked if he felt sad.

"It's not a sad day," he replied, "but it's a very emotional day. I tried to prepare myself for this, but once you sign the papers that say you've retired, once you get up there and tell the people, it's a little bit different. I've decided to go to a new life, but I'm going to miss this life. I've been on a high for 17 years."

He did admit that he was fighting off tears. "The reason I'm making so many jokes," he confessed, "is to save myself from crying."

So Bird quipped his way through the difficult moments. But across pro basketball, there weren't many belly laughs.

"The Bulls regret this is one of the saddest days in NBA history with the retirement of Larry Bird," said Chicago general manager Jerry Krause in a prepared release.

From the Cleveland Cavaliers, the pronouncements were almost funereal. "We have lost one of the true legends of our time," said center Brad Daugherty.

"The game has lost one of the greatest players of all time," agreed his coach, Lenny Wilkens.

"Pro basketball has just thrown away the mold," Pat Riley, then coach of the Knicks, said. "He was one of a kind... unique... Not just the best of the best, but the only one who did what he did. He was a true warrior."

"It's kind of like when Alexander the Great decided he wasn't going to conquer any more countries," observed Indiana Pacers president Donnie Walsh.

Still, few were truly surprised by the announcement. Bird had played with the "Dream Team" in the 1992 Summer Olympic Games in Barcelona, and while his effort there was inspired, it was also hindered by his back pain.

His Olympic teammates sensed that the games he played with them might be his last. "When Larry retires, that's it," Magic told reporters during the Olympics. "He'll be gone from the game, and we won't get to see what he does anymore. There were great ones before him, and there'll be great ones after. But there will never, ever, never be another Larry Bird."

"I know the time I spent with Larry on the so-called Dream Team was special," said Chicago's Michael Jordan.

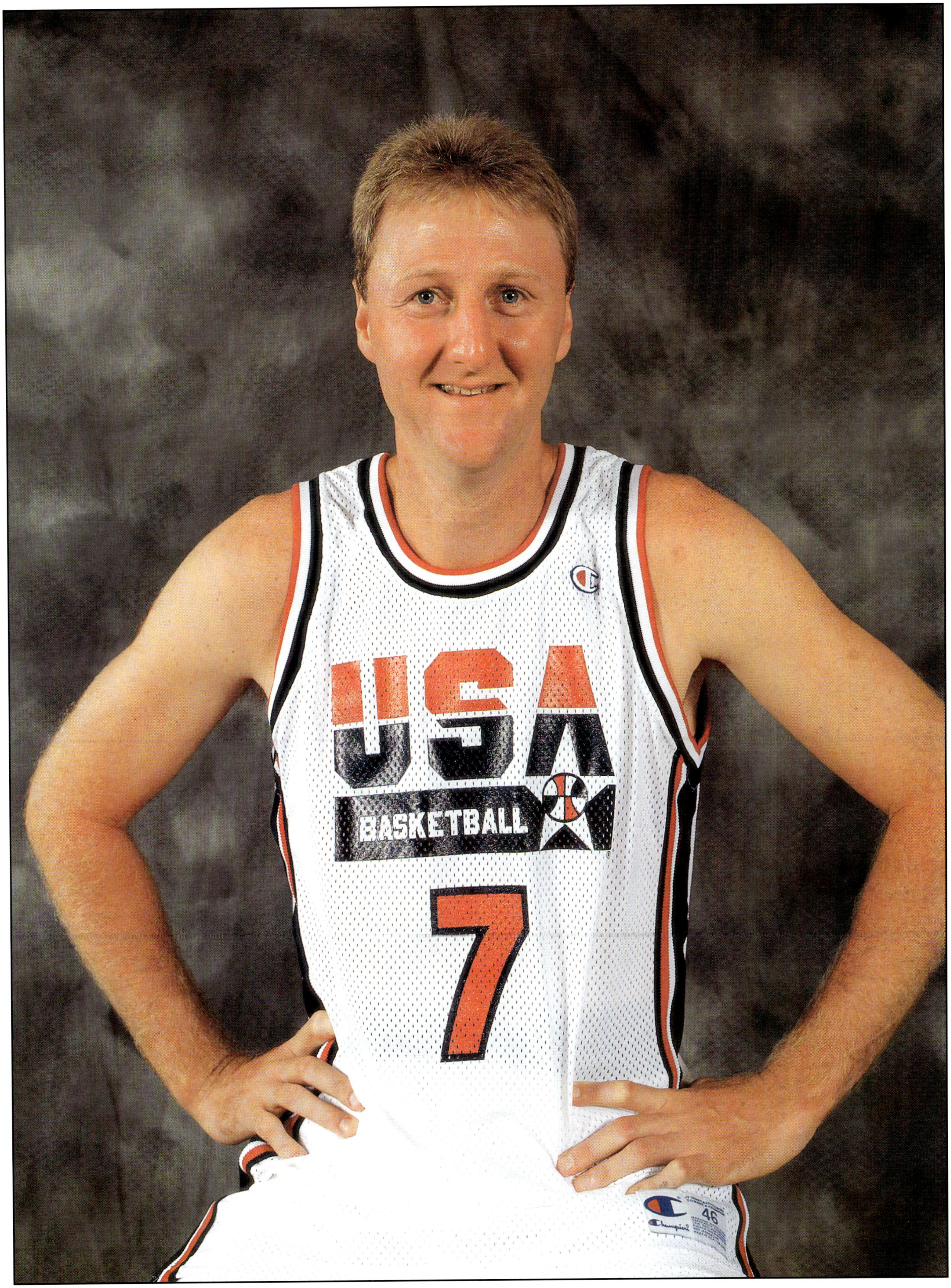
USA
BASKETBALL
7

Bird saved a special respect for Red Auerbach.

Bird with life-sized wooden statue by artist Armand La Montagne.

BIRD: Portrait of a Competitor

"He was one of the greatest players ever and a great leader, and to be able to play with him fulfills one of my dreams."

In his time, Bird had fulfilled the dreams of millions.

"I remember me and D.J. would be sitting on the bench at the end of a game," he recalled. "And I'd look up and say, 'I just can't believe 15,000 people would come to watch us play.' I never could understand it. I never will understand it."

Yet Bird did understand. He drew his energy from the Garden crowd and took great pleasure before big games in asking the fans to help boost the Celtics through the tough spots. "All I ask of the fans," he once explained, "is to be vocal, to keep it loud, to pick it up if they see we're a little fatigued and to get us over the hump."

They got each other over the hump, Larry and his fans.

Asked how he wanted to be remembered, Bird quipped, "That he didn't weigh as much as everyone thought he would."

Turning serious, he added, "One thing I know, I played as hard as I could every time I was out there. I wasn't going to let an injury stop me from diving on the floor for a loose ball. I had to compete at a high level. I played one way—as hard as I could—and my body held up pretty well over the years. I played in over 1,100 games. I gave my heart, body and soul for the Celtics. I hope that's how they remember me."

He said he didn't want the fanfare of retirement, but he would be eager to see his number "33" hanging in the Garden rafters with the other Celtic greats.

The Celtics also announced that he would stay with the organization as a special assistant to Gavitt. With his retirement, Bird gave up $3.75 million in salary he was slated to receive for the season, but those close to him said that he had banked $20 million or more over the years. He had once predicted that he would leave Boston someday with every penny he had ever earned. And he had.

"If I had a healthy back now, I'd play for nothing," he said.

No one doubted him.

At the end of the press conference, Dave Gavitt stepped back to the rostrum and called for champagne to make one final toast to Larry. He then turned and called for someone to fill a glass for Bird.

"How 'bout a beer?" said the Hick from French Lick with a grin.

The room broke into a final round of laughter.

Which is just the way he wanted to go out.

"This is the greatest life in the world," he said. "If you know how to play basketball, it's the easiest game in the world. Don't feel sorry for me. I had a great life the last 17 years. I've had nothing but highs."

But Celtics fans everywhere weren't feeling sorry for him. They were feeling sorry for themselves.

"Without Magic and without Bird, I don't think the Celtics-Lakers rivalry will be as intense," said Jim Caton, a Laker fan in Los Angeles. "When we play Boston now, I don't really feel the sense of competition. It's a huge swing from the old dynasties, the Lakers and Boston. The torch has been passed."

Leroy Nieman and his Larry Bird.

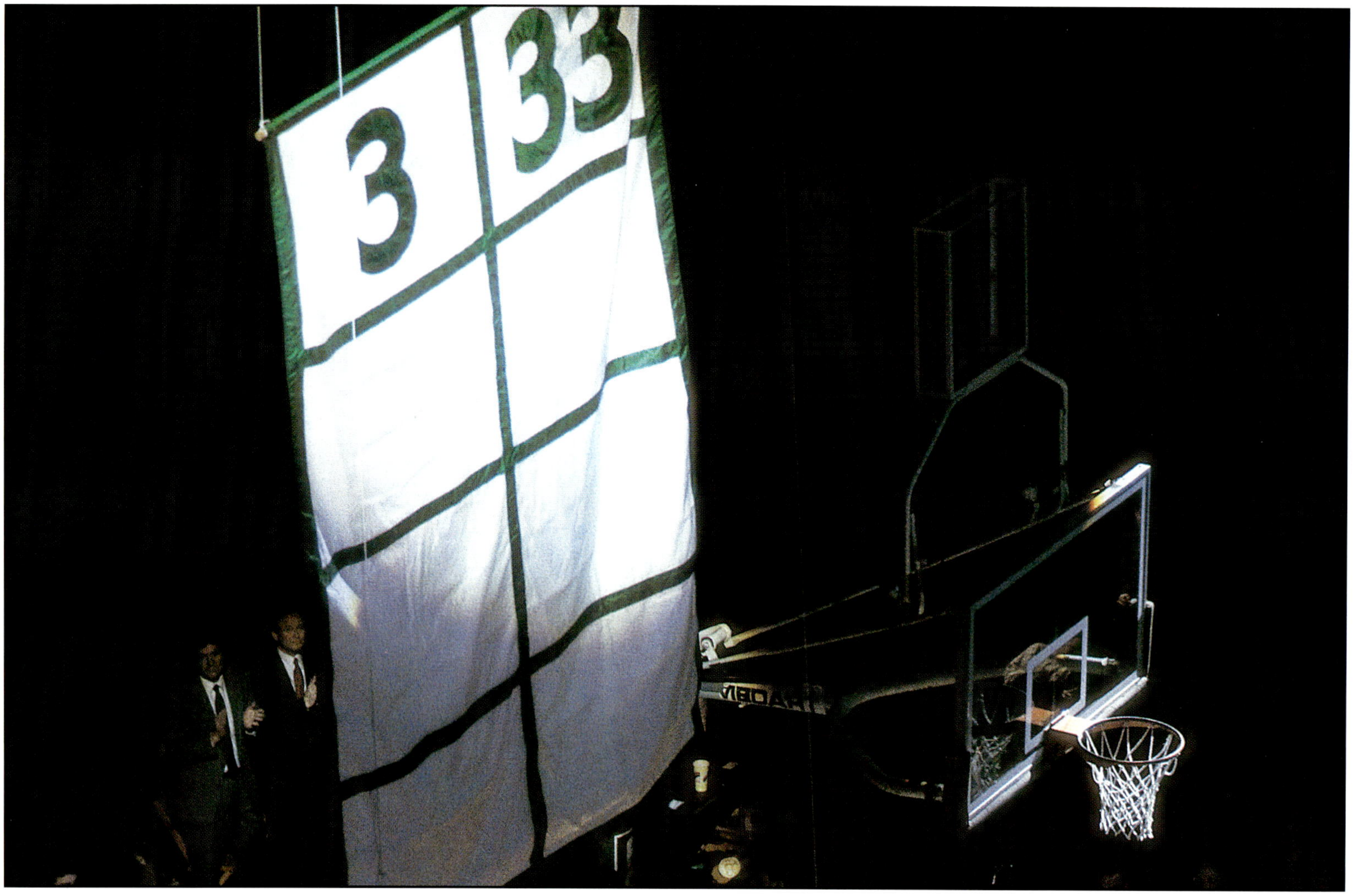
3
33

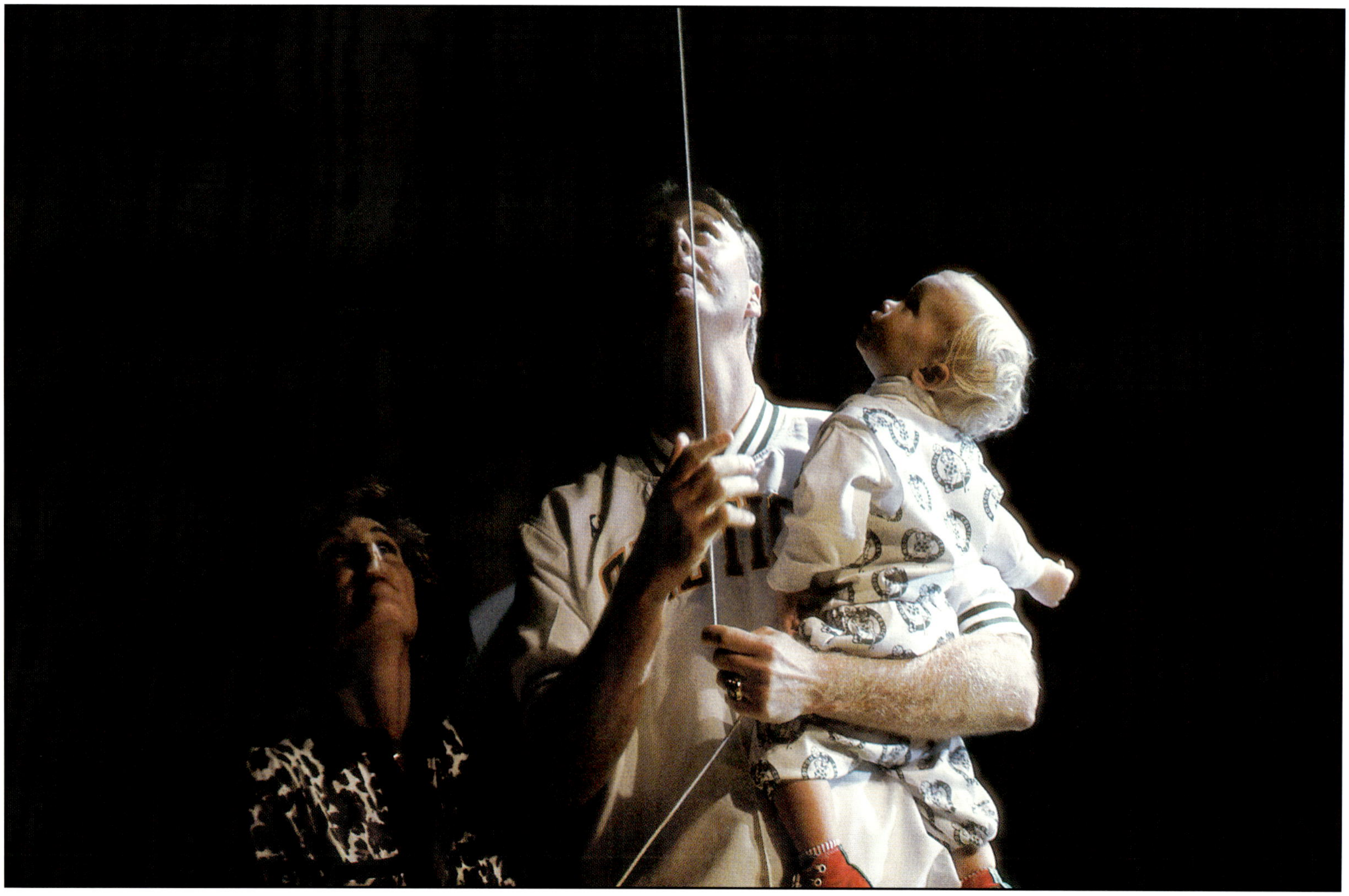

Larry leaves the Garden after playing his last game there.

VI Indiana

As a player, Bird once mentioned that after retiring from pro basketball he might like to coach a high school team. Many of those around him suggested that such a scenario would be impossible. Yet it was just the kind of thought that reminded you of his refrain, "I'm the type of guy who surprises people."

Few at the time could forsee him ever becoming a pro coach. But, then again, few at that time could ever forsee an era in which NBA coaches were pulling down $4 million or more per season. Certainly the dollars played a role in Bird's decision to accept the coaching job with the Indiana Pacers. But a bigger factor was his love of the game and his desire to be around it.

His role in management with the Celtics had produced little satisfaction. And his days at home in Florida lacked the clear purpose he'd known as a player. The golf was fun, but it didn't go nearly far enough in filling the empty hours.

In short, Larry's work ethic was bubbling with nothing to really cook up.

That changed immediately when he took over the Pacers.

"I've got a lot of work to do," was one of his first pronouncements. So then he went about doing it.

His return home to Indiana caused quite a stir in the hoops-crazy state. So reporters asked him about it. "I don't really get involved in that stuff, because I had so much of it over my career," he said of the fan mania. "I just sort of like to stand in the background. But it has caused a lot of excitement, which I'm happy for, because at least people are still interested in what I'm doing. I'm back home, coaching a professional team in my home state. I'm excited about that."

Like former teammate Chris Ford, Bird has taken on the anxiety of coaching.

His Pacers roster was filled with solid veterans, and Bird made it clear from the start what he expected of them. "We're going to run a lot, because I feel that the only way you can play the game of basketball the way that it's supposed to be played is if you're in top condition," he said. "As a player for 20-some years, I always prided myself on staying in pretty good condition, and during the season in top condition. That's the only way you can perform at your highest level. You're able to do things if you're in top condition. You can't do 'em if you're not."

Under coach Larry Brown a season earlier, the Pacers had finished 39-43 and didn't even make the playoffs, meaning that expectations were modest when Bird took over. Still, the anxiety level jumped when the club got off to a 2-5 start. Bird was so angry after an early loss in Charlotte that he hardly could speak with the press. But from there, the Pacers righted themselves and rushed off to the best record in the NBA's Eastern Conference over the first half of this season, a performance that netted Bird the honor of coaching the Eastern Conference team in the 1998 NBA All-Star Game in New York.

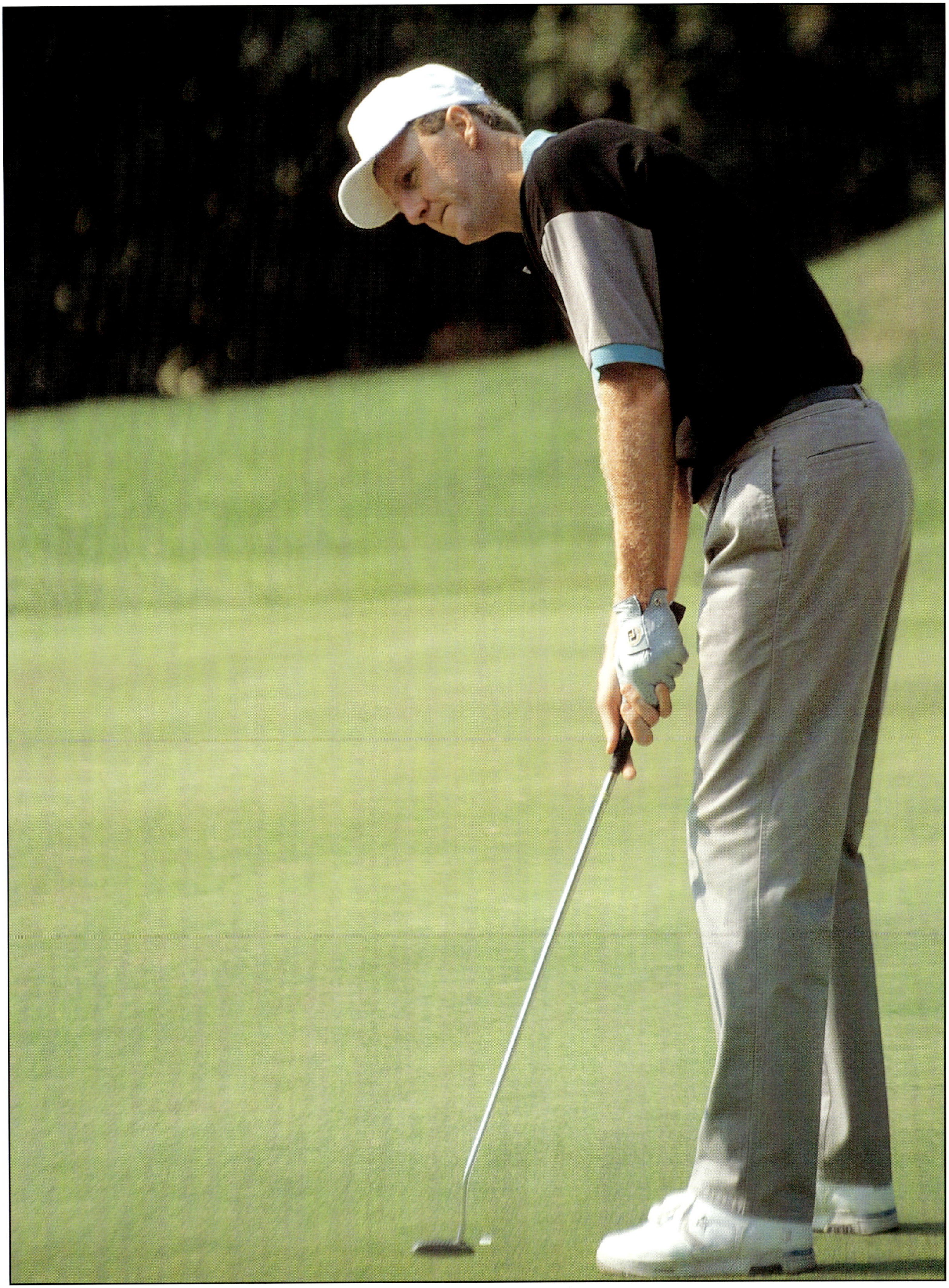

BIRD: Portrait of a Competitor

Much of his success could be attributed to Bird's ability to relate to his players, something that observers had at first suggested would be a problem. It was theorized that because he was a basketball legend, Bird might have trouble understanding less talented people playing for him. But just the opposite proved to be the case.

"It's definitely an honor and a privilege to play for him," Indiana point guard Travis Best said, "but I'm past all the legend-type stuff. He's fun to play for. He's low-key, but when you look at him he portrays someone who is in control. ... Last year, we'd go into games feeling like we were going to win, but at the same time when we'd get out there it was just like we were dead. Now we go in knowing we're going to win. It doesn't matter if we're down 10 points or up two points. We know we're going to win."

Bird treated his players with respect and avoided the yelling and screaming that precipitates conflict between NBA players and coaches. "He's not going to rant and rave on the sideline," explained Pacers guard Mark Jackson said. "He knows how to get his point across and get things done. At the same time, he talks like he's in the Celtics' locker room ... That's the difference. Former players who try coaching have somewhat of an ego and say, This is the way you do it because that's the way I did it. (Bird) comes in with none of that. He wants to teach and he's done a phenomenal job."

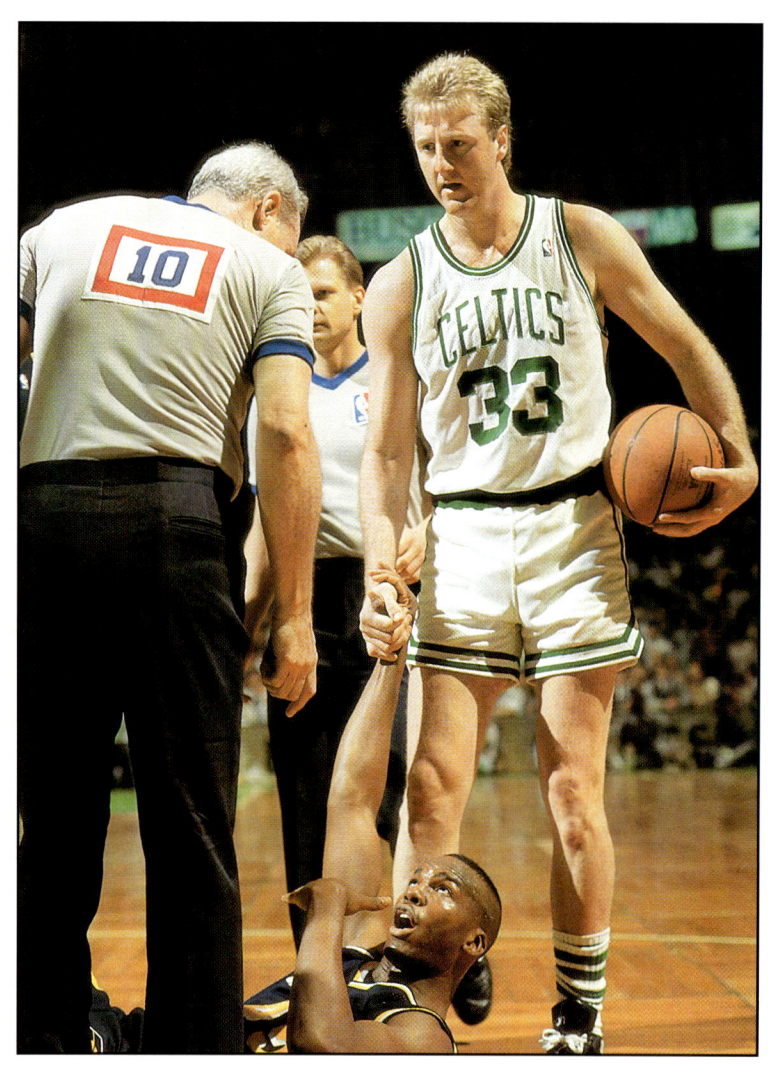

"It's not what he says, it is how he says it that is making the difference," Best said. "He doesn't scream at you, he doesn't embarrass you when you make a mistake. He just looks at you, and you get the message. Then when the time is right, he'll talk to you calmly and explain what he wants."

Veteran Reggie Miller, the team's scoring leader, pointed out that Bird focused on preparation in practice, but during the games, he let his players play. "That's probably been his greatest attribute," Miller said.

It has helped that Bird has an experienced team, populated with veterans who used to compete against Bird. Miller, the shooting guard, used to attempt to outblast Bird when Indiana faced the Celtics. Rik Smits provided a solid scoring option at center. Jackson had a reputation as a dependable point guard, much like Dennis Johnson used to help Bird run the Celtics. And vetern Chris Mullin, brought in from Golden State in an offseason trade, gave the Pacers a steady small forward who can score, like Bird himself.

Bird won the team over by spreading the workload across the roster. He let nine players play more than 22 minutes a game. And he showed a strong inclination to admit his mistakes.

"I'm still learning about each one of these guys," Bird said of his players. "Derrick McKey never says a word, so I don't know anything about him. But you learn about these

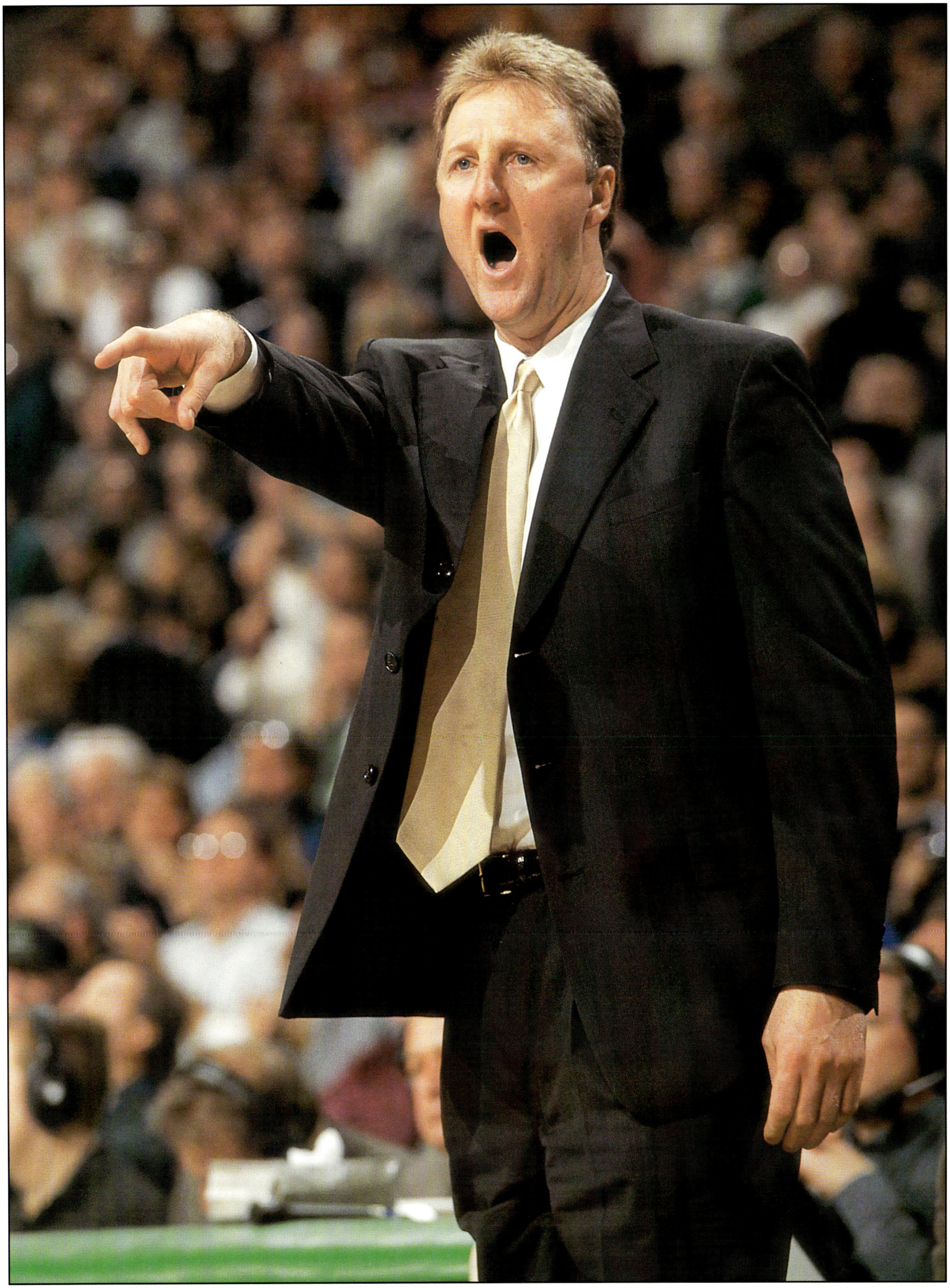

BIRD: Portrait of a Competitor

guys when you're on the road with them or watching them in practice. These guys have been excellent to work for. And I say I work for them, because it's their team. I just try and put people in the right places."

That means the Pacers are taking a relaxed approach, having fun and winning games. "I think it is easier," Miller said. "Guys can relax, and not always have to be looking at the bench to see if they did anything wrong."

Bird, for his part, says the game belongs to the players. "The one comment that he made, that made me understand that he had a clue, was that coaching is overrated, and that's the truth," Jackson said. "You take your players, allow them to get into the best condition, the best shape possible. You give them the x's and o's, you prepare them, you have fun, and on game days you trust them to come up with results. You give them confidence and then you sit there and relax like you're a genius. He's done a wonderful job of that."

"You learn being on the road with them, watch them around practice, and in games. You try and learn what you can about them," Bird said of his players. "As ballplayers they've done everything I've asked. They've been excellent to work for. I always say I work for them, because it's their team. It is up to them if they want to go out and give the effort every night."

Although the Pacers lacked defensive quickness, they are one of the NBA's best defensive teams, because of team effort and hard work. Bird has focused on defense in long practices. "You don't mind long practices when it shows in results, and we're getting that," scoring leader Reggie Miller said. "He makes practices fun. You know what he wants, and he has a way of telling you with a smile."

As far as motivating his players, Bird told reporters that the presence of Red Auerbach in Boston Garden had always motivated him, because Auerbach was always recalling some great feat that one or another of the Celtics had accomplished.

Bird stopped short of saying that he hoped his own presence would inspire the people he coached, but he implied that was his wish.

"His record proves he knows the game of basketball," said Mark Jackson. "We're all young enough that we've seen him play and know about his dedication. We know he can make us win, and we work to get the job done."

There were high hopes for Bird in 1979 when he came into the league. Making few promises, he was a college senior when he told reporters, "I've been working hard for a long, long time. And I'll tell you the truth: I never dreamed I'd be where I am today But I know what got me here: I gave 100 percent of myself, and that's never going to stop."

From Larry Bird, that's all the promise the folks in Indiana will ever need.

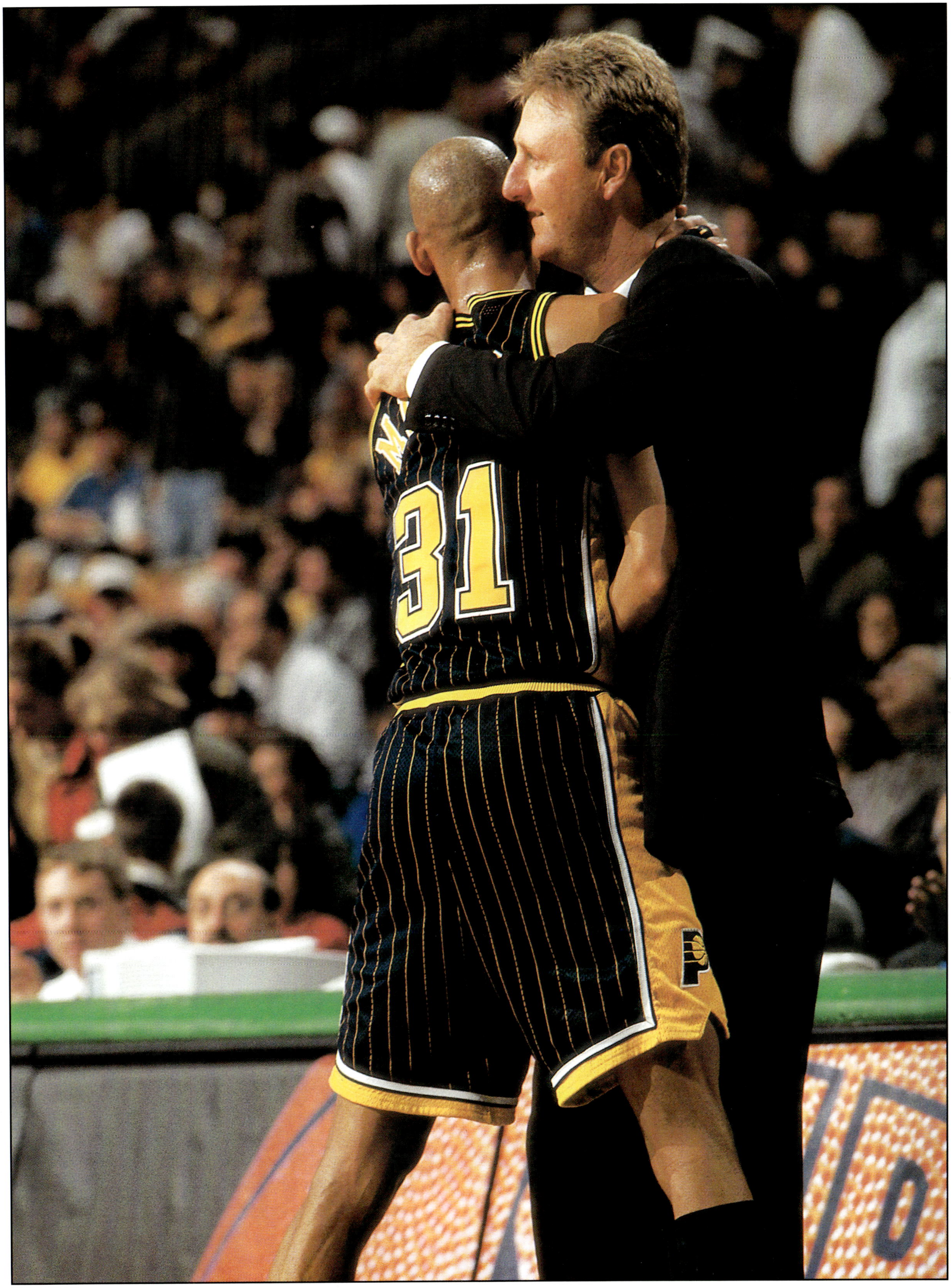
31

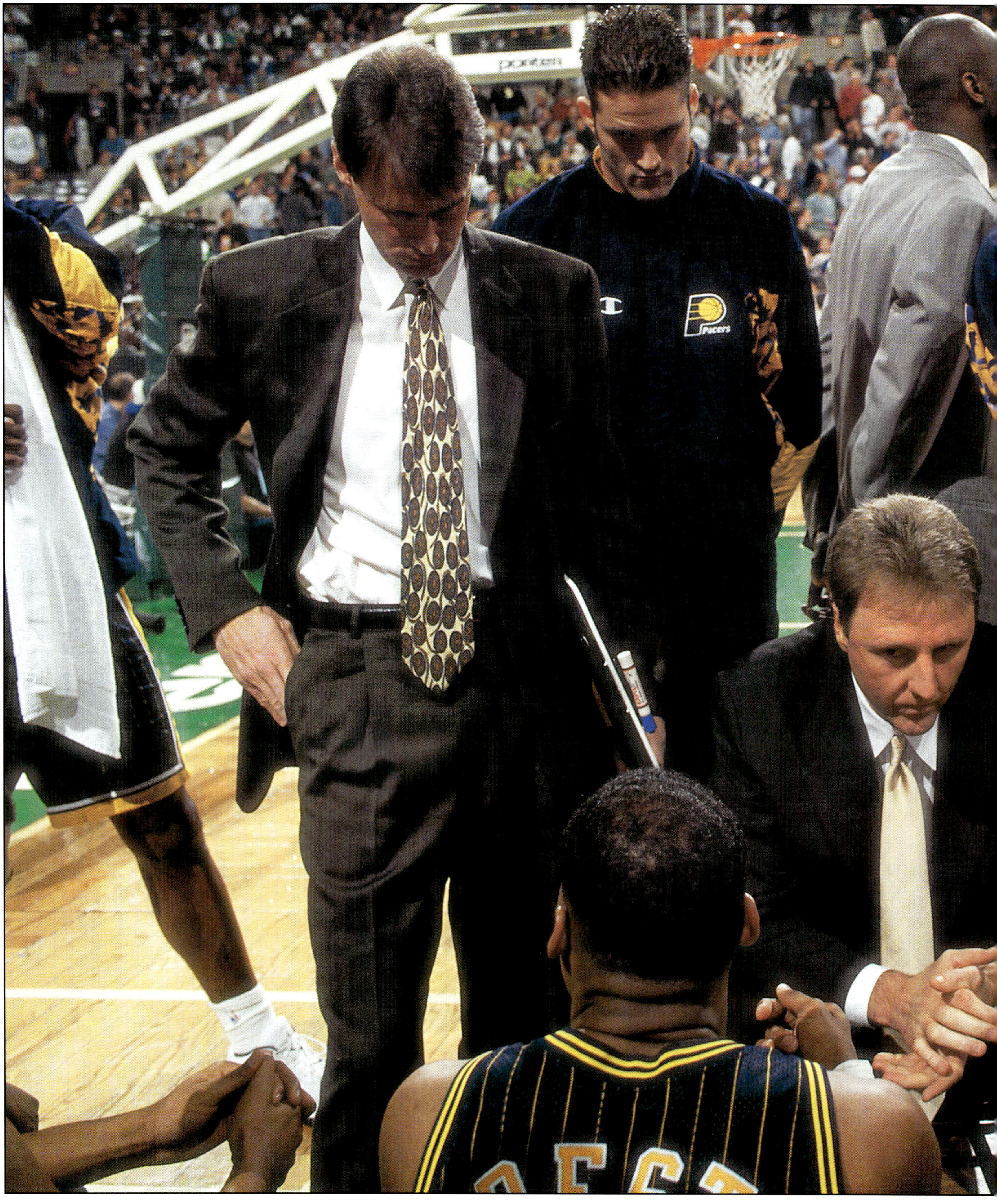
Pacers

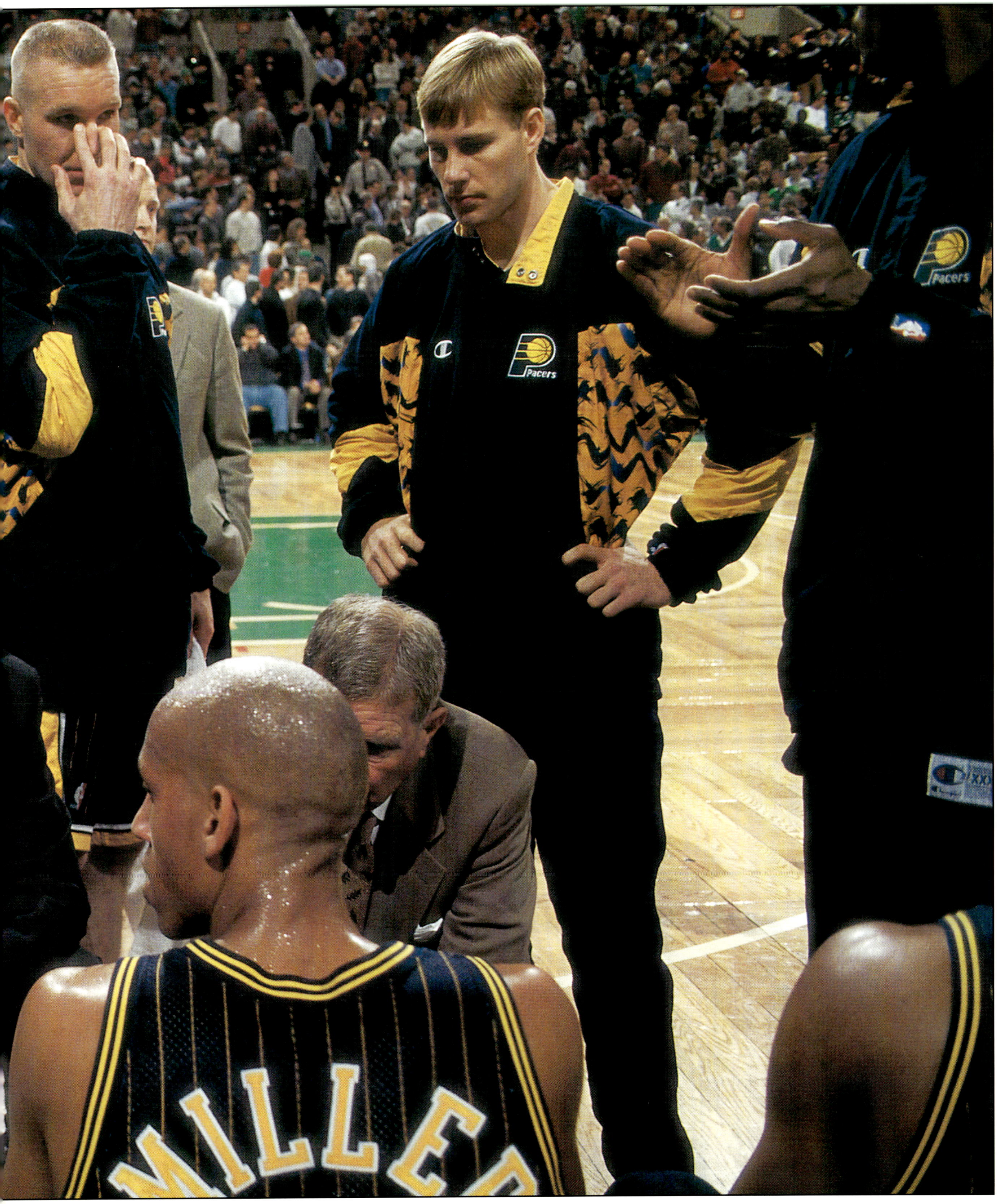
Pacers

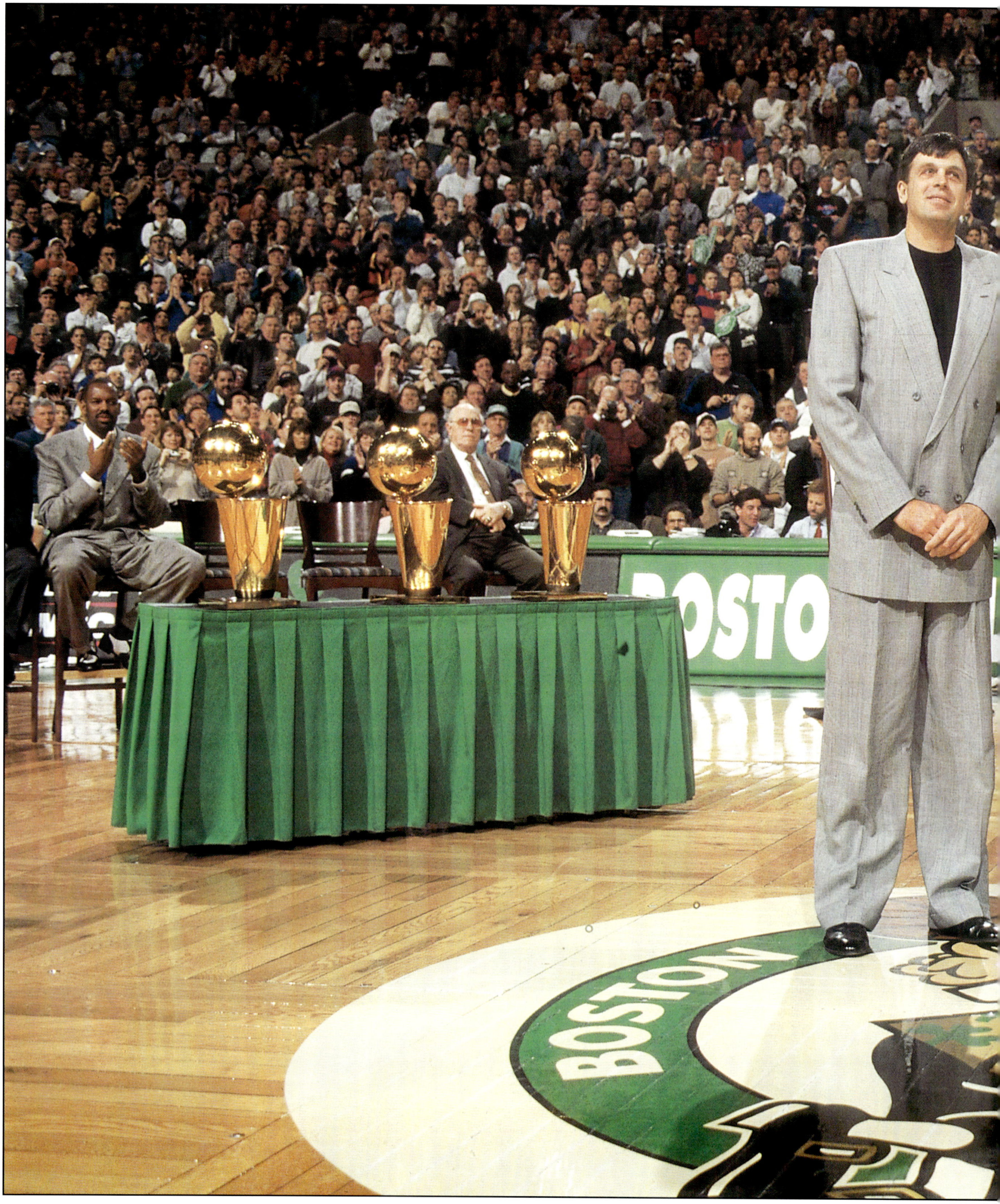
BOSTON
BOSTON

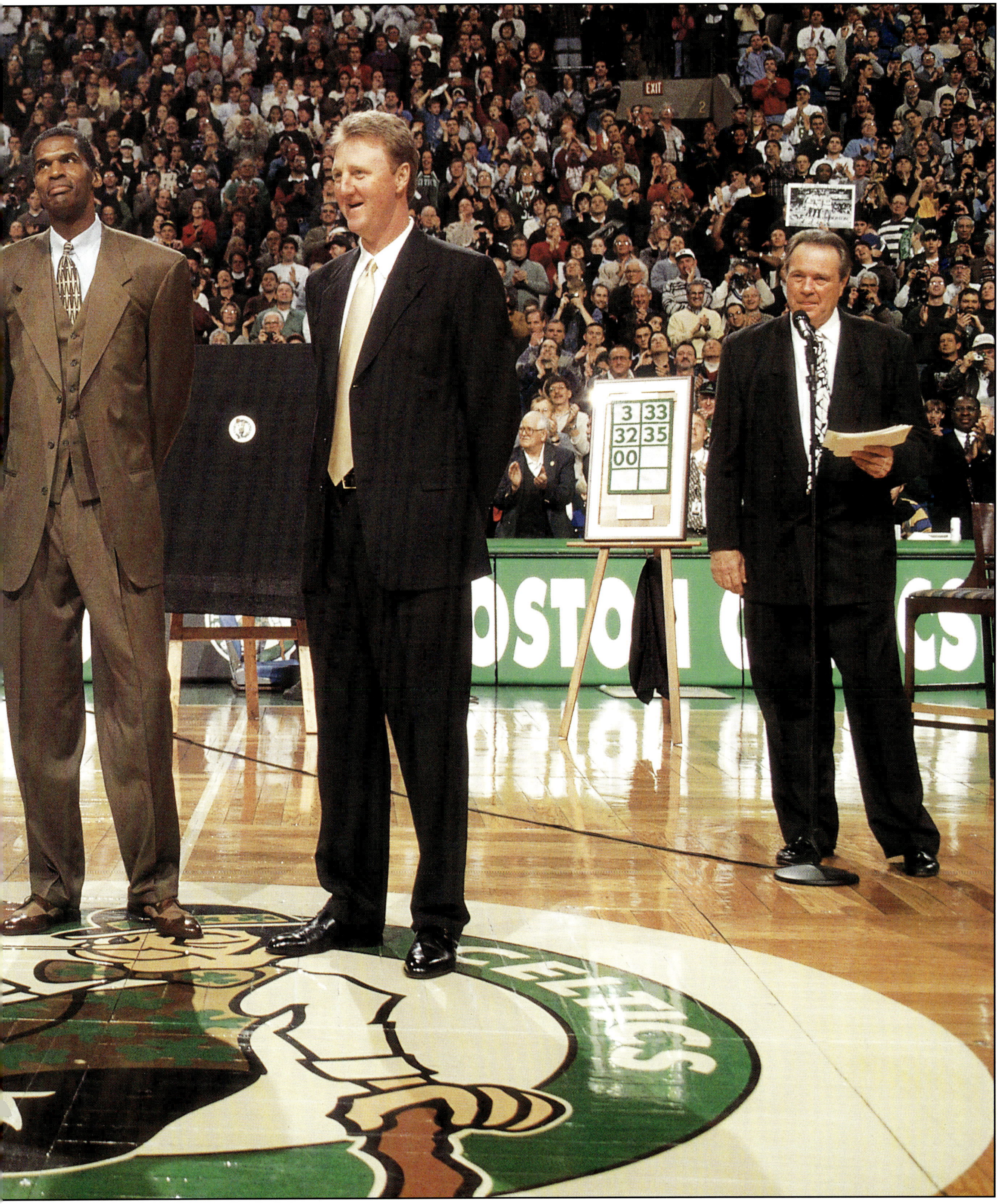
EXIT
3
33
32
35
00
CELTICS

Great Performances

- February 1981 at the Forum in Los Angeles, in the middle of a spirit-breaking road trip. Bird racks up 36 points, 21 rebounds, five steals and six assists to lead Boston to the win over Magic and the Lakers.

- March 1983, Bird answers a loss to the Pacers in Indiana one night by scoring 53 against them the next night in Boston Garden.

- The 1984 playoffs, Game 7 vs. Bernard King and the Knicks at Boston Garden. Bird's numbers? 12 rebounds, 10 assists and 39 points.

- Game 5 vs. the Lakers in the 1984 NBA Finals. The game was crucial and so was Larry, with 34 points and 17 rebounds. He hit 15 of 20 from the floor.

- The Bourbon Street Blast, in New Orleans against the Atlanta Hawks in March 1985. Bird scores 60, just nine days after Kevin McHale had set a new team single-game scoring record with 57.

- Valentine's Day, 1985, when Bird broke hearts in Portland in overtime, totalling 47 points, 14 rebounds and 11 assists.

- The Steal (who doesn't know about this one?), in Game 5 of the 1987 Eastern Finals, when Larry ripped off an Isiah Thomas pass to feed Dennis Johnson for the winning layup.

- Game 7 of the 1988 Eastern semifinals vs. Atlanta, when Dominique Wilkins scored 47 in the Garden, but the Legend finished with 20 in the fourth quarter to drive Boston to the next round.

- The Lazarus Act of 1992, when Bird fought off back pain to score 49 with 12 assists and 14 rebounds in 54 minutes of a triple-overtime win over Portland in the Garden.

BIRD: Portrait of a Competitor

Bird's Top Regular Season Performances

Points	Rebounds	Assists
60 vs. Atl. at N.O. (3-12-85)	21 at Washington (3-16-82)	17 at Golden State (2-16-84)
53 vs. Indiana (3-30-83)	21 at Denver (12-29-81)	16 vs. Cleveland (3-21-90)
50 vs. Dallas (3-10-86)	21 at LA Lakers (2-11-81)	15 vs. Washington (4-1-87)
50 vs. Atlanta (11-10-89)	21 at Philadelphia (11-1-80)	15 vs. Cleveland (3-27-85)
49 vs. Washington (1-27-88)	20 six times	15 vs. Atlanta (1-13-82)
49 at Phoenix (2-15-88)		15 vs. Cleveland (11-2-90)
49 vs. Portland (3-15-92)		

Regular Season Record

Year	Team	G	Min	FGM	FGA	Pct.	FTM	FTA	Pct.	Off	Def	Tot	Ast	PF-Dq	St	Bl	Pts	Avg
79-80	Bos.	82	2955	693	1463	.474	301	360	.836	216	636	852	370	279-4	143	53	1745	21.3
80-81	Bos.	82	3239	719	1503	.478	283	328	.863	191	704	895	451	239-2	161	63	1741	21.2
81-82	Bos.	77	2923	711	1414	.503	328	380	.863	200	637	837	447	244-0	143	66	1761	22.9
82-83	Bos.	79	2982	747	1481	.504	351	418	.840	193	677	870	458	197-0	148	71	1867	23.6
83-84	Bos.	79	3028	758	1542	.492	374	421	.888	181	615	796	520	197-0	144	69	1908	24.2
84-85	Bos.	80	3161	918	1760	.522	403	457	.882	164	678	842	531	208-0	129	98	2295	28.7
85-86	Bos.	82	3113	796	1606	.496	441	492	.896	190	615	805	557	182-0	166	51	2115	25.8
86-87	Bos.	74	3005	786	1497	.525	414	455	.910	124	558	682	566	185-3	135	70	2076	28.1
87-88	Bos.	76	2965	881	1672	.527	415	453	.916	108	595	703	467	157-0	125	57	2275	29.9
88-89	Bos.	6	189	49	104	.471	18	19	.947	1	36	37	29	18-0	6	5	116	19.3
89-90	Bos.	75	2944	718	1517	.473	319	343	.930	90	622	712	562	173-2	106	61	1820	24.3
90-91	Bos.	60	2277	462	1017	.454	163	183	.891	53	456	509	431	118-0	108	58	1164	19.4
91-92	Bos.	45	1662	353	758	.466	150	162	.926	46	388	434	306	82-0	42	33	908	20.2
TOTALS		897	34443	8591	17334	.496	3960	4471	.886	1757	7217	8974	5695	2279-11	1556	755	21791	24.3

Three-Point Field Goals: 1979-80, 58-for-143 (.406); 1980-81, 20-for-74 (.270); 1981-82, 11-for-52 (.212); 1982-83, 22-for-77 (.286); 1983-84, 18-for-73 (.247); 1984-85, 56-for-131 (.427); 1985-86, 82-for-194 (.423); 1986-87, 90-for-225 (.400); 1987-88, 98-for-237 (.414); 1988-89, 0-for-0 (.000); 1989-90, 65-for-195 (.333); 1990-91, 77-for-198 (.389); 1991-92, 52-for-128 (.406); Totals: 649-for-1727 (.376).

Playoff Record

Year	Team	G	Min	FGM	FGA	Pct.	FTM	FTA	Pct.	Off	Def	Tot	Ast	PF-Dq	St	Bl	Pts	Avg
79-80	Bos.	9	372	83	177	.469	22	25	.880	22	79	101	42	30-0	14	8	192	21.3
80-81	Bos.	17	750	147	313	.470	76	85	.894	49	189	238	103	53-0	39	17	373	21.9
81-82	Bos.	12	490	88	206	.427	37	45	.822	33	117	150	67	43-0	23	17	214	17.8
82-83	Bos.	6	240	49	116	.422	24	29	.828	20	55	75	41	15-0	13	3	123	20.5
83-84	Bos.	23	961	229	437	.524	167	190	.879	62	190	252	136	71-0	54	27	632	27.5
84-85	Bos.	20	815	196	425	.461	121	136	.890	53	129	182	115	54-0	34	19	520	26.0
85-86	Bos.	18	770	171	331	.517	101	109	.927	34	134	168	148	55-0	37	11	466	25.9
86-87	Bos.	23	1015	216	454	.476	176	193	.912	41	190	231	165	55-1	27	19	622	27.0
87-88	Bos.	17	763	152	338	.450	101	113	.894	29	121	150	115	45-0	36	14	417	24.5
88-89	Bos.	0	0	0	0	0	0	0	0	0	0	0	0	0	0	0	0	0
89-90	Bos.	5	207	44	99	.444	29	32	.906	7	39	46	44	10-0	5	5	122	24.4
90-91	Bos.	10	396	62	152	.408	44	51	.863	8	64	72	65	28-0	13	3	171	17.1
91-92	Bos.	4	107	21	42	.500	3	4	.750	2	16	18	21	7-0	1	2	45	11.3
TOTALS		164	6886	1458	3090	.472	901	1012	.890	360	1323	1683	1062	466-1	296	145	3897	23.8

Three-Point Field Goals: 1979-80, 4-for-15 (.267); 1980-81, 3-for-8 (.375); 1981-82, 1-for-6 (.167); 1982-83, 1-for-4 (.250); 1983-84, 7-for-17 (.412); 1984-85, 7-for-25 (.280); 1985-86, 23-for-56 (.411); 1986-87, 14-for-41 (.341); 1987-88, 12-for-32 (.375); 1988-89, 0-for-0 (.000); 1989-90, 5-for-19 (.263); 1990-91, 3-for-21 (.143); 1991-92, 0-for-5 (.000)
Totals: 80-for-249 (.321)

All-Star Game Record

Year	Team	Min	FGM	FGA	Pct.	FTM	FTA	Pct.	Off	Def	Tot	Ast	PF-Dq	St	Bl	Pts	Avg
1980	Bos.	23	3	6	.500	0	0	.000	3	3	6	7	1-0	1	0	7	7.0
1981	Bos.	18	1	5	.200	0	0	.000	1	3	4	3	1-0	1	0	2	2.0
1982	Bos.	28	7	12	.583	5	8	.625	0	12	12	5	3-0	1	1	19	19.0
1983	Bos.	29	7	14	.500	0	0	.000	3	10	13	7	4-0	2	0	14	14.0
1984	Bos.	33	6	18	.333	4	4	1.000	1	6	7	3	1-0	2	0	16	16.0
1985	Bos.	31	8	16	.500	5	6	.833	5	3	8	2	3-0	0	1	21	21.0
1986	Bos.	35	8	18	.444	5	6	.833	2	6	8	5	5-0	7	0	23	23.0
1987	Bos.	35	7	18	.389	4	4	1.000	2	4	6	5	5-0	2	0	18	18.0
1988	Bos.	32	2	8	.250	2	2	1.000	0	7	7	1	4-0	4	1	6	6.0
1990	Bos.	23	3	8	.375	2	2	1.000	2	6	8	3	1-0	3	0	8	8.0
1991	Bos.— selected, did not play due to back injury —																
1992	Bos.— selected, did not play due to back injury —																
TOTALS:		287	52	123	.423	27	32	.844	19	60	79	41	28-0	23	3	134	13.4

Three-Point Field Goals: 1980, 1-for-2 (.500); 1983, 0-for-1 (.000); 1985, 0-for-1 (.000); 1986, 2-for-4 (.500); 1987, 0-for-3 (.000); 1988, 0-for-1 (.000); 1990, 0-for-1 (.000). Totals: 3-for-13 (.231)

Season/Career Highs

	FGM	FGA	FTM	FTA	REB	AST	ST	BL	PTS
1991-92/Regular Season	19/22	35/36	14/16	14/17	19/21	12/17	4/9	2/5	49/60
1992/Playoffs	8/17	18/33	2/14	2/15	6/21	14/16	1/62/4		16/43

Ejections

Date	Opponent	Score	Points	Minutes
11-12-86	vs. Milwaukee	W/124-116	2	9
02-17-86	at Phoenix	L/101-108	24	30
11-19-84	vs. Philadelphia	W/130-119	42	30
03-11-83	at New Jersey	L/93-98	8	25
02-03-81	at Utah	L/89-104	25	35

20 Rebounds Efforts
(regular season and playoffs)

Date	Opponent	Score	Points	Rebounds
11-01-80	at Philadelphia	L/113-117	36	8-13-21
12-13-80	at Chicago	W/106-95	35	2-18-20
12-20-80	at Cleveland	W/107-102	21	6-14-20
12-25-80	at New York	W/117-108	28	3-17-20
04-23-80	at Philadelphia	L/97-99	22	2-19-21
02-11-81	at Lakers	W/105-91	36	5-16-21
05-07-81	vs. Houston	L/90-92	19	4-17-21
12-29-81	at Denver	W/123-128	27	7-14-21
03-16-81	at Washington	W/98-97 (OT)	31	5-16-21
02-04-81	at Indiana	W/102-93	23	6-14-20
04-13-84	at Detroit	W/120-128 (OT)	29	4-16-20
06-06-84	at Lakers	W/129-125 (OT)	29	9-12-21
04-11-87	vs. Indiana	W/120-106	42	4-16-20

Disqualifications

Date	Opponent	Score	Points	Mins
10-19-79	at Indiana	L/128-131	20	22
12-15-79	at New York	W/99-96	31	43
01-29-79	at Chicago	W/103-99	14	31
02-08-80	vs. Indiana	W/130-108	14	23
10-14-80	at Atlanta	L/116-122	19	42
11-12-80	vs. Washington	W/93-86	15	32
11-22-86	at Atlanta	L/96-97	18	44
12-10-86	vs. New Jersey	W/108-98	35	30 (reserve)
04-03-87	vs. Detroit	W/119-115	31	33
02-02-90	at Minnesota	L/105-116	18	36
02-23-90	at Golden State	W/123-111	25	41

BOSTON
CELTICS
NBA
1984
WORLD
CHAMPIONS
BOSTON
CELTICS
NBA
1981
WORLD
CHAMPIONS
BOSTON
CELTICS

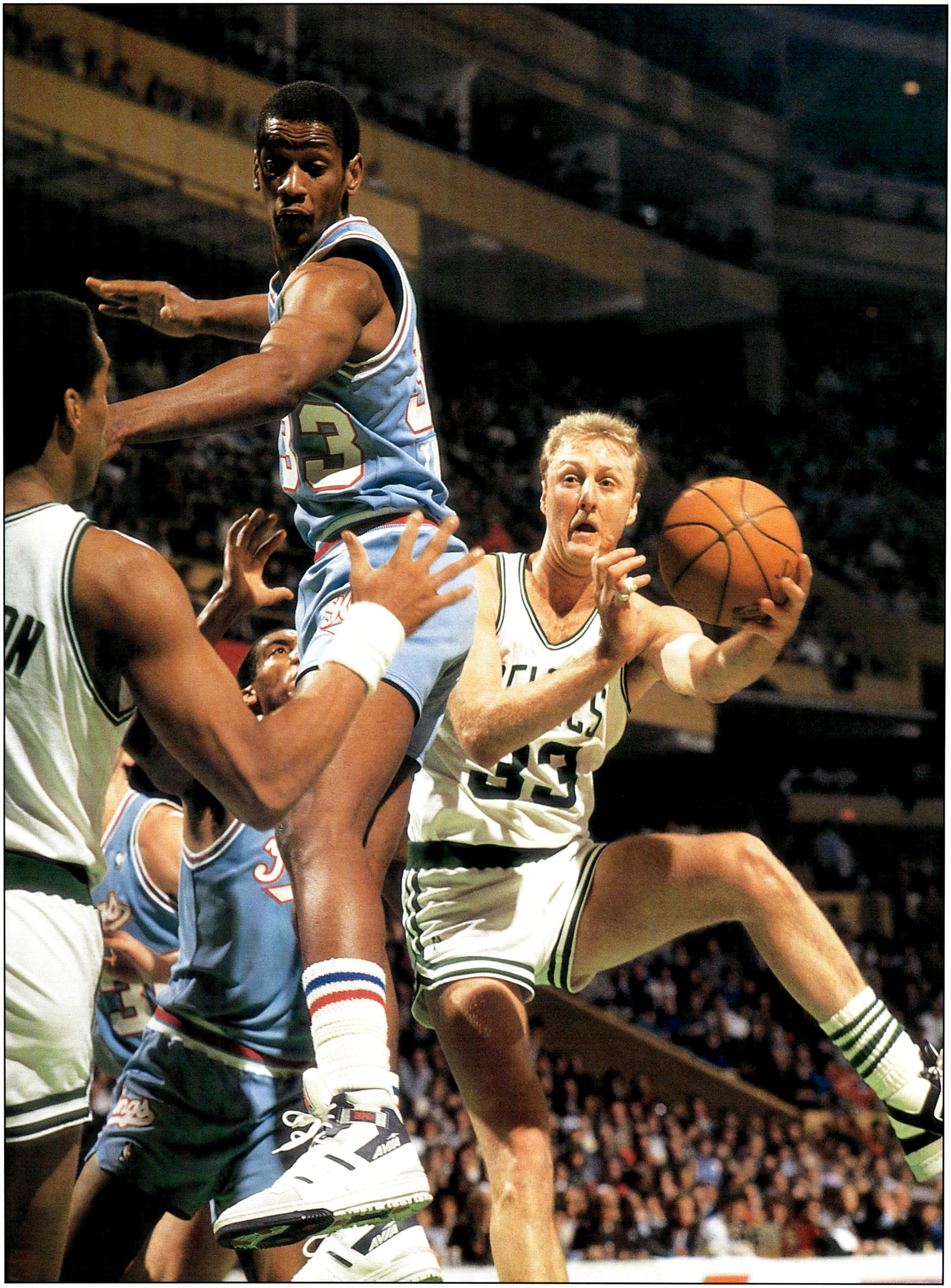

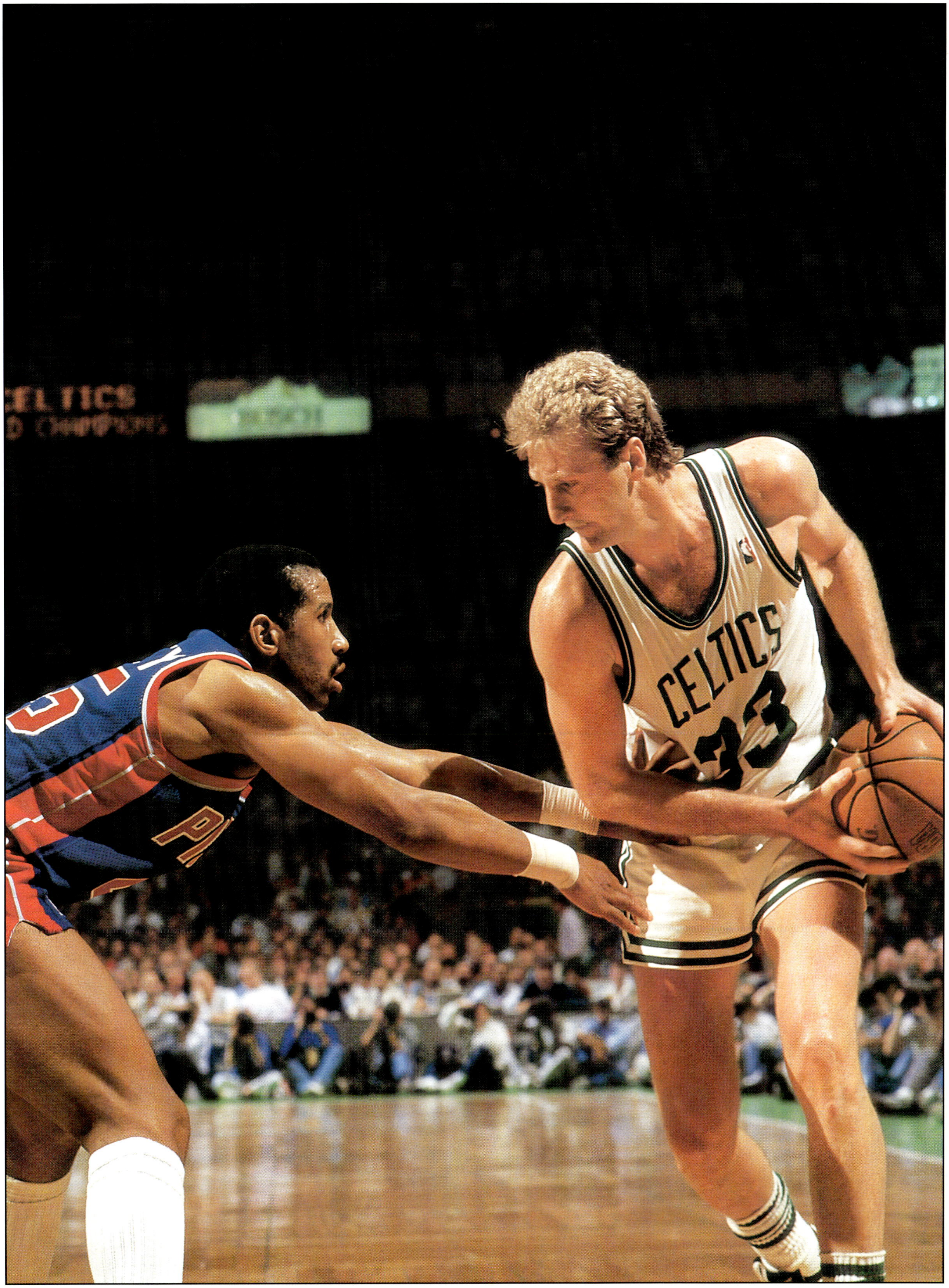
CELTICS
CELTICS

BIRD: Portrait of a Competitor

Larry Bird's Career Triple Doubles

x-playoffs   *-consecutive games

Season	No.	Team	Site	Date	Reb	Ast	Pts	Score
1979-80	1	Detroit	Home	11-14	19	10	23	115-111
1980-81	6	*Phoenix	Away	12-30	10	10	27	116-97
		*San Diego	Away	1-1	13	10	13	88-85
		Utah	Home	1-21	10	10	20	117-87
		Indiana	Away	3-6	10	10	28	104-110
		New York	Away	3-24	13	10	16	118-116
		xChicago	Away	4-10	17	10	24	113-107
1981-82	5	*New Jersey	Away	1-11	14	10	25	112-94
		*Atlanta	Home	1-13	19	15	28	116-95
		Seattle	Away	2-21	12	14	22	100-103
		xPhila	Home	5-9	15	10	24	121-81
		xPhila	Away	5-15	13	11	15	113-121
1982-83	4	Detroit	Away	12-4	16	12	30	119-112
		Utah	Away	1-1	15	11	14	127-112
		San Anton	Away	1-7	12	10	25	116-113
		Washington	Away (OT)	4-2	10	12	34	121-117
1983-84	8	Denver	Away	11-15	11	10	28	140-124
		New York	Away (2)	11-22	11	11	16	113-117
		San Anton	Home	11-30	14	13	23	130-106
		Phila	Home	12-4	11	13	22	114-121
		Houston	Home	2-10	14	12	17	114-101
		Seattle	Away	2-17	13	13	30	111-100
		Chicago	Home	4-8	10	10	30	117-110
		xNew York	Home	5-13	12	10	39	121-104
1984-85	8	*Phoenix	Away	12-26	11	10	34	119-114
		*LAC	Away	12-27	13	13	13	118-103
		*San Anton	Away	12-29	15	10	18	120-112
		New York	Away	1-7	10	10	26	108-97
		Utah	Away	2-18	12	10	30	110-94
		*Detroit	Home	3-3	15	10	30	138-129
		*New York	Away	3-5	19	10	20	110-102
		Milwaukee	Home	3-20	13	11	10	107-105
1985-86	13	New Jersey	Away (OT)	10-25	12	10	21	109-113
		New York	Away	11-23	10	10	18	113-104
		*Seattle	Away	2-13	15	11	31	107-98
		*Portland	Away (OT)	2-14	14	11	47	120-119
		Golden St.	Away	2-19	12	11	36	115-110
		*Indiana	Home	2-23	11	12	30	113-98
		*New York	Away	2-25	18	13	24	91-74
		LAC	Home	2-28	13	12	20	124-108
		Detroit	Home	4-2	11	13	29	122-106
		Phila	Away	4-6	10	10	18	94-95
		xMilwaukee	Away	5-17	16	13	19	111-107
		xHouston	Away	6-1	15	11	25	104-106
		xHouston	Home	6-8	11	12	29	114-97
1986-87	6	Atlanta	Away (OT)	2-3	15	14	26	123-126
		Dallas	Away	2-18	12	11	16	113-96
		Phila	Home	3-29	13	12	17	118-100
		Washington	Home	4-1	17	15	30	103-86
		Phila	Away (OT)	4-5	10	12	39	104-106
		xMilwaukee	Home	5-19	16	11	18	104-91
1987-88	2	San Anton	Away	2-10	17	10	39	136-120
		Milwaukee	Home	4-13	10	10	26	123-104
1988-89	0							
1989-90	11	New Jersey	Home	11-15	15	10	12	126-92
		Charlotte	Away	12-5	13	11	11	114-101
		Denver	Home	12-8	12	12	24	102-103
		Seattle	Home	12-13	11	10	40	109-97
		Sacramento	Away (OT)	12-27	11	10	37	115-112
		Orlando	Away	1-17	10	10	14	133-111
		*New Jersey	Home	3-18	18	11	29	122-106
		*Cleveland	Home	3-21	10	16	25	123-114
		Cleveland	Away	4-6	15	10	11	109-104
		New York	Home	4-15	17	13	17	101-94
		xNew York	Home	4-26	18	10	24	116-105
1990-91	4	Miami	Home	11-26	14	11	21	118-101
		Atlanta	Home	12-23	10	10	14	132-104
		LA Lakers	Away	2-15	11	11	11	98-85
		xIndiana	Home	4-26	12	12	21	127-120
1991-92	1	Portland (2)	Home	3-15	14	12	49	152-148

20,000 Points and 5,000 Assists in NBA R/S Career

Larry Bird joined an exclusive club of individuals who have registered 20,000 points and 5,000 assists in their regular season NBA career. A breakdown of what the five individuals have accomplished follows:

	Jabbar	Robertson	West	Havlicek	Bird
TOTALS					
Points	38,387	26,710	25,192	26,395	21,791
Assists	5,660	9,887	6,238	6,114	5,695
Years	20	14	14	16	13
Games	1,560	1,040	932	1,270	897

BIRD: Portrait of a Competitor

Regular Season 40+ Point Efforts in the Larry Bird Era

SEASON	PLAYER	OPPONENT	SITE	DATE	PTS	MINS	SCORE
79-80	Larry Bird	Phoenix	Phoenix	2-13-80	45	43	134-135
	Larry Bird	Detroit	Boston	3-2-80	41	44	118-115
80-81	Robert Parish	San Antonio	San Antonio	2-17-81	40	33	128-116
81-82	Larry Bird	Detroit	Boston	1-10-82	40	45	134-124
82-83	Larry Bird	Indiana	Boston	3-30-83	53	33	142-116
83-84	Larry Bird	Portland	Boston	12-2-83	41	45	115-106
84-85	Larry Bird	Atlanta	New Orl	3-12-85	60	43	126-115
	Kevin McHale	Detroit	Boston	3-3-85	56	41	138-129
	Larry Bird	Atlanta	Boston	12-9-84	48	42	128-127
	Larry Bird	Portland	Boston	1-27-85	48	45	128-127
	Larry Bird	Houston	Boston	3-17-85	48	43	134-120
	Larry Bird	Milwaukee	Boston	4-12-85	47	38	113-115(OT)
	Larry Bird	Indiana	Indiana	2-24-85	45	45	113-100
	Larry Bird	Philadelphia	Boston	11-9-84	42	30	130-119
	Kevin McHale	New York	New York	3-5-85	42	44	110-102
	Larry Bird	Dallas	Dallas	11-27-84	40	44	114-99
	Larry Bird	Denver	Denver	2-20-85	40	46	129-132
85-86	Larry Bird	Dallas	Dallas	3-10-86	50	40	115-116
	Larry Bird	Detroit	Boston	11-27-85	47	39	132-124
	Larry Bird	Portland	Portland	2-14-86	47	49	120-119(OT)
	Larry Bird	Cleveland	Hartford	3-18-86	43	29	126-96
	Larry Bird	Atlanta	Atlanta	1-18-86	41	40	125-122(OT)
	Larry Bird	New Jersey	Boston	3-30-86	40	46	122-117
86-87	Larry Bird	New York	Boston	4-12-87	47	38	119-107
	Larry Bird	Portland	Boston	2-25-87	43	46	122-116
	Larry Bird	Seattle	Boston	3-20-87	42	46	112-108
	Larry Bird	Chicago	Chicago	3-27-87	41	46	111-106
	Larry Bird	Atlanta	Boston	1-23-87	40	39	126-106
	Larry Bird	New Jersey	Boston	3-22-87	40	42	116-104
87-88	Larry Bird	Washington	Boston	1-27-88	49	43	106-100
	Larry Bird	Phoenix	Phoenix	2-15-88	49	43	107-106
	Larry Bird	Washington	Washington	11-7-87	47	53	140-139(2OT)
	Larry Bird	Houston	Houston	2-9-88	44	44	120-129
	Larry Bird	Portland	Boston	2-24-88	44	44	113-112
	Larry Bird	Chicago	Boston	4-21-88	44	40	126-119
	Larry Bird	Indiana	Boston	11-11-87	42	42	120-106
	Larry Bird	Golden State	Golden State	1-2-88	41	43	115-110
	Larry Bird	New York	Boston	1-6-88	41	44	117-108
	Larry Bird	Denver	Boston	12-9-87	40	40	119-124
	Larry Bird	Portland	Portland	2-19-88	40	40	124-104
88-89	Danny Ainge	Philadelphia	Boston	12-9-88	45	37	121-107
89-90	Larry Bird	Atlanta	Boston	11-10-89	50	39	117-106
	Larry Bird	Orlando	Orlando	3-16-90	46	44	130-127
	Larry Bird	New Jersey	Boston	4-6-90	43	45	125-106
	Larry Bird	Philadelphia	Boston	3-11-90	41	43	107-105
	Larry Bird	Seattle	Boston	12-13-89	40	46	109-97
	Larry Bird	Utah	Boston	12-20-89	40	41	113-109
	Larry Bird	Miami	Boston	4-12-90	40	40	139-118
90-91	Larry Bird	Charlotte	Boston	11-14-90	45	44	135-126
	Larry Bird	Denver	Boston	12-5-90	43	44	148-140
91-92	Larry Bird	Portland	Boston	3-18-82	49	54	152-148(2OT)

BIRD: Portrait of a Competitor

BOSTON CELTICS vs. LA LAKERS — BIRD vs. MAGIC

Includes Regular Season and Playoff Games

				- Larry Bird -			- Johnson -	
Date	Site	Score	Pts	Ast	Reb	Pts	Ast	Reb
12/28/79	LAL	LAL 123-105	16	3	4	23	6	8
01/13/80	Bos	LAL 100-98	14	1	12	1	2	3
01/18/81	Bos	Bos 98-96	11	5	9	Did Not Play		
02/11/81	LAL	Bos 105-91	36	6	21	Did Not Play		
02/07/82	Bos	LAL 119-113	11	9	10	Did Not Play		
02/14/82	LAL	Bos 108-103	12	9	9	19	8	10
01/30/83	Bos	Bos 110-95	21	8	13	14	10	9
02/23/83	LAL	Bos 113-104	32	9	17	20	10	13
02/08/84	Bos	LAL 111-109	29	7	11	20	10	8
02/24/84	LAL	LAL 116-108	14	5	11	9	18	8
05/27/84	Bos	LAL 115-109	24	5	14	18	10	6
05/31/84	Bos	Bos 124-121	27	3	13	27	9	10
06/03/84	LAL	LAL 137-104	30	2	7	14	21	11
06/06/84	LAL	Bos 129-125	29	2	21	20	17	11
06/08/84	Bos	Bos 121-103	34	2	17	10	13	5
06/10/84	LAL	LAL 119-108	28	8	14	21	10	6
06/12/84	Bos	Bos 111-102	20	3	12	16	15	5
01/16/85	Bos	Bos 104-102	19	7	11	8	13	7
02/17/85	LAL	LAL 117-111	33	3	15	37	13	3
05/27/85	Bos	Bos 148-114	19	9	6	19	12	1
05/30/85	Bos	LAL 109-102	30	3	12	14	13	4
06/02/85	LAL	LAL 136-111	20	3	7	17	16	9
06/05/85	LAL	Bos 107-105	26	5	11	20	12	11
06/07/85	LAL	LAL 120-111	20	7	7	26	17	6
06/09/85	Bos	LAL 111-100	28	3	10	14	14	10
01/22/86	Bos	Bos 110-95	21	7	12	15	6	0
02/16/86	LAL	Bos 105-99	22	7	18	6	12	6
12/12/86	Bos	LAL 117-110	26	6	3	31	8	7
02/15/87	LAL	LAL 106-103	20	7	5	39	10	7
06/02/87	LAL	LAL 126-113	32	6	7	29	13	8
06/04/87	LAL	LAL 141-122	23	4	10	22	20	5
06/07/87	Bos	Bos 109-103	30	4	12	32	9	11
06/09/87	Bos	LAL 107-106	21	7	10	29	5	8
06/11/87	Bos	Bos 123-108	23	7	12	29	12	8
06/14/87	LAL	LAL 106-93	16	5	9	16	19	8
12/11/87	Bos	LAL 115-114	35	8	9	18	17	8
02/14/88	LAL	LAL 115-106	25	4	17	22	14	5
12/16/88	Bos	Bos 110-96	Did Not Play		31	7	3	
02/19/89	LAL	LAL 119-110	Did Not Play		Did Not Play			
12/15/89	Bos	LAL 119-110	21	2	12	16	21	6
02/18/90	LAL	LAL 116-110	20	7	7	30	13	4
01/27/91	Bos	LAL 104-87	Did Not Play		22	15	9	
02/15/91	LAL	Bos 98-85	11	11	11	21	16	9
11/29/91	Bos	Bos 114-91	22	7	10	Did Not Play		
02/16/92	LAL	Bos 114-107	Did Not Play		Did Not Play			
Career Totals: LAL Lead 25-20			951	226	458	795	486	276
Career Averages:			23.2	5.5	11.2	20.4	12.5	7.1

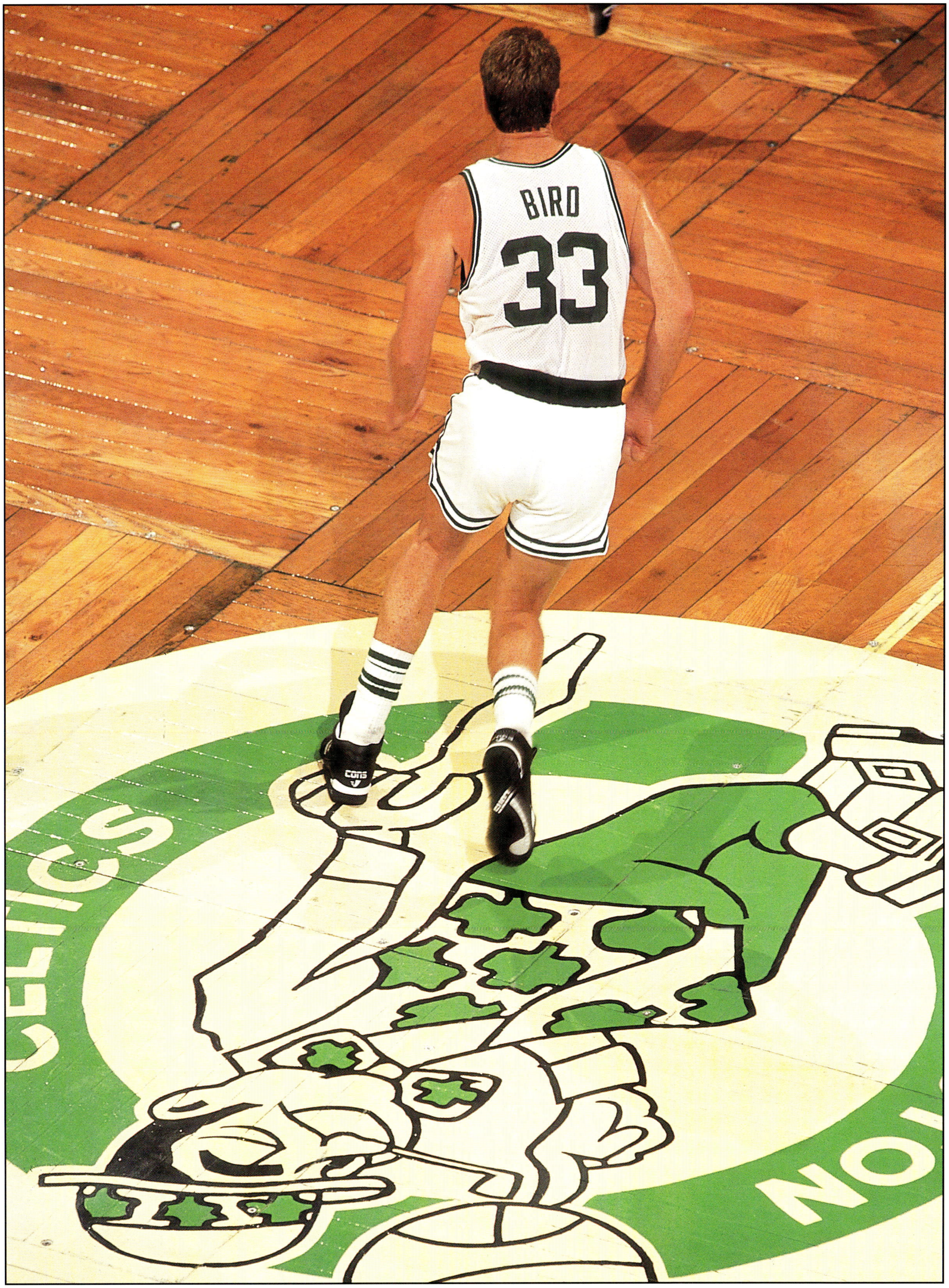
BIRD
33
CELTICS

BIRD: Portrait of a Competitor

Acknowledgments

For most of Larry Bird's career as an NBA player, it was my privilege to sit courtside at the Boston Garden as photographer for the Boston Celtics. I wouldn't have traded that seat for anything in the world.

If I hadn't been there to take his picture, Larry may still have had some success, but had Larry not been there, I know that I would have missed out on some of the greatest experiences of a lifetime. Thanks, Larry.

- S.L.

Thank goodness for Larry Bird and all the fun he has created for basketball fans over the years, first as a player, then as a coach. Thank goodness, too, for Jeff Twiss and the Celtics' excellent media relations staff, and the outstanding Boston-area sportswriters who have provided first-rate information about the team over the years. Without their work over the years, compiling a tribute book such as this would be nearly impossible. In addition to my own interviews and observations, I have consulted a wide array of sources in preparing the essay to accompany Steve Lipofsky's excellent photography.

- R.O.L.

Sources include the following:

Magazines and Newspapers

Extensive use was made of a variety of publications, including the *Baltimore Sun*, *Basketball Times*, *Boston Globe*, *Boston Herald*, *Brockton Enterprise*, *Chicago Tribune*, *Chicago Sun Times*, *The Detroit News*, *The Detroit Free Press*, *Flint Journal*, *Hartford Courant*, *Hoop Magazine*, *Houston Post*, *Los Angeles Times*, *L.A. Herald Examiner*, *The National*, *New York Daily News*, *The New York Times*, *New York Post*, *The Oakland Press*, *The Roanoke Times & World-News*, *The Charlotte Observer*, *USA Today*, *The National*, *The Orange County Register*, *The Oregonian*, *Patriot Ledger*, *Philadelphia Inquirer*, *Sport*, *Sports Illustrated*, *The Sporting News*, *Street & Smith's Pro Basketball Yearbook*, and *The Washington Post*.

The Writers

Without the front-line work of a variety of reporters and writers over the years, the compilation of this history would have been greatly hampered. In most cases in the text, these people are referred to as "the writers."

That group includes the following: Bob Ryan, Joe Fitzgerald, Roy S. Johnson, Donald Hall, Alan Goldstein, Larry Donald, Jack Madden, Tony Kornheiser, Ted Green, Dave Kindred, Mitch Chortkoff, Pat Putnam, Sandy Padwe, Jack McCallum, Sam McManis, Doug Cress, Mike Littwin, John Papanek, Sam Goldaper, George Vecsey, Alex Wolff, Bruce Newman, Jackie MacMullan, Steve Bulpett, Peter May, Mike Fine, Frank Dell'Apa, Will McDonough, Ailene Voisin, Jim Fenton, Bob Schron and numerous others. Photos on pages 106 and 124 by Winslow Townson / Lipofsky Assoc. Banner Photo page 106 by Andy Ryan / Lipofsky Assoc.

Books

50 Years of the Final Four by Billy Packer and Roland Lazenby
Basketball for the Player, the Fan and the Coach by Red Auerbach
Bird, The Making of An American Sports Legend by Lee Daniel Levine
Cousy on the Celtic Mystique by Bob Cousy and Bob Ryan
Drive, The Story of My Life, by Larry Bird and Bob Ryan
Forty-Eight Minutes by Bob Ryan and Terry Pluto
Magic's Touch by Magic Johnson and Roy S. Johnson
Rebound by K.C. Jones and Jack Warner
Red on Red by Red Holzman and Harvey Frommer
Showtime, by Pat Riley and Byron Laursen
Sportswit by Lee Green
The Bird Era by Bob Schron and Kevin Stevens
The Bob Verdi Collection by Bob Verdi
The Boston Celtics by Bob Ryan
The Boston Celtics Greenbook, 1988-89 and 1989-90, by Roland Lazenby
The Jim Murray Collection by Jim Murray
The Mickey Herskowitz Collection by Mickey Herskowitz
The Official NBA Basketball Encyclopedia, edited by Zander Hollander and Alex Sachare
The Story of Basketball by Dave Anderson
Winnin' Times by Scott Ostler and Steve Springer